In Search of Maryland Ghosts

Montgomery County

Karen Yaffe Lottes

and Dorothy Pugh

4880 Lower Valley Road • Atglen, PA 19310

Published by Schiffer Publishing, Ltd.
4880 Lower Valley Road
Atglen, PA 19310
Phone: (610) 593-1777; Fax: (610) 593-2002
E-mail: Info@schifferbooks.com

For the largest selection of fine reference books on this and related subjects,
please visit our website at: **www.schifferbooks.com.**
You may also write for a free catalog.

This book may be purchased from the publisher.
Please try your bookstore first.

We are always looking for people to write books on new and related subjects.
If you have an idea for a book, please contact us at
proposals@schifferbooks.com

Schiffer Books are available at special discounts for bulk purchases for sales promotions or premiums. Special editions, including personalized covers, corporate imprints, and excerpts can be created in large quantities for special needs. For more information contact the publisher.

In Europe, Schiffer books are distributed by
Bushwood Books
6 Marksbury Ave.
Kew Gardens
Surrey TW9 4JF England
Phone: 44 (0) 20 8392 8585; Fax: 44 (0) 20 8392 9876
E-mail: info@bushwoodbooks.co.uk
Website: www.bushwoodbooks.co.uk

Other Schiffer Books on Related Subjects:
Ghosts and Haunted Houses of Maryland, 978-0-8703-3382-8, $8.95
Ghosts of Maryland, 978-0-7643-3423-8, $14.99

Copyright © 2012 by Karen Lottes and Dorothy Pugh
Unless otherwise noted, images are the property of the authors.

Library of Congress Control Number: 2012941743

All rights reserved. No part of this work may be reproduced or used in any form or by any means—graphic, electronic, or mechanical, including photocopying or information storage and retrieval systems—without written permission from the publisher.

The scanning, uploading and distribution of this book or any part thereof via the Internet or via any other means without the permission of the publisher is illegal and punishable by law. Please purchase only authorized editions and do not participate in or encourage the electronic piracy of copyrighted materials.

"Schiffer," "Schiffer Publishing, Ltd. & Design," and the "Design of pen and inkwell" are registered trademarks of Schiffer Publishing, Ltd.

Designed by Mark David Bowyer
Type set in Amulet / New Baskerville BT

ISBN: 978-0-7643-4010-9
Printed in the United States of America

Contents

Dedication

To the ghosts who inspired us.

To my children Mira and Jered, whose enthusiasm over uncovering tombstones was contagious, and my husband John, who was very supportive of this project at a difficult time in my life.

— Karen Yaffe Lottes

To my family for their love and support through this whole adventure: Mike, Anna G., Bo, Marjie, Greg, Michele, Robbie, Joey, and especially to Anna P. for her story, and to Lori, for reading stories and giving valuable suggestions.

— Dorothy Pugh

Acknowledgments

There are so many people to thank that it has been hard for us to keep track. First, we especially need to thank all the contributing authors: Joanna Church, Vivian Eicke, Barbara Finch, Clarence Hickey, Jeff Penn, Anna Pickard, Ken Ruback, Susan Soderberg, and Meg Williams. Their stories help give the book a more varied and interesting voice.

There were many people who helped us with research or shared the stories of their homes unselfishly. First, we are especially grateful to Patricia Andersen, Jane Sween, and the Library Ladies at the Montgomery County Historical Society's Jane C. Sween Library. They gave research help and moral support almost weekly as the project developed. Also, Clare Kelly and Kevin Manarolla of the Montgomery County Historic Preservation Commission, Stephanie Brown at the Chevy Chase Historical Society, and Margaret Wentz and the staff of the Sandy Spring Museum. Mike Dwyer was one of our go-to historical resources.

We also interviewed and asked for help from many people: Bill Allman; Andred; Jerry and Patricia Antonuccio; Jim Archer; Joanne Atay; Heather Bouslog and the staff and volunteers at Needwood; Leonard Becraft; Jan Broulik and Joey Phillips; the staff at the Capitol Historian's Office; Emily Cavey; James Caywood; Joey Caywood; Isabel Church; Lou Church; Bill and Diane Conway; Mary Charlotte Crook; Susan Demory; Denise Gibbs; Walt Goetz; the volunteers and staff at Great Falls Tavern; Esther Henning; Perry Kapsch; Sheila Keenan; Kevin at Camp Bennett; Alexis Lang; Kathy Lehman; Mary Lou Luff; Karen McFarland; Lisa McKillop; Thene and George Mernick; Janet Millenson; Georgianne Mitchell; Jean Moyer; Mark Myers; Linda and Henry Nessul; David Neumann; Janice and Samuel Nicholson; Bill and Eda Offutt; Charles Overly; Dave Phillips, Pam Phillips, and Christian Newcomer; Susan and Dick Piper; Betty Ponds; James Ricciuti; William Robertson; Beth Rodgers; Pete Sante; James Sorenson; Katherine Stevens; Adriana and Carlos Torres; Chris Wilkinson; Mary Wolfe; the Zeender Family; Robin Ziek; and last but not least, those sources who chose to remain anonymous.

Finally, this project has been a labor of love and might not have happened had we not had a community of support behind us. First, we are grateful to our families: John, Mira, and Jered Lottes; Mike Pugh and Anna Greco; Lori Pugh and Bo, Marjie, and Anna Pickard; and Greg, Michele, Robbie, and Joey Pugh. They gave us moral support as well as occasionally trudging through underbrush and reading and writing stories. Also, our cheering squad and sometime reviewers: Lauren Yaffe, Elissa Cohen, Marc and Cynthia Yaffe, Mary Kay Harper, Jennie Cottrell, Joanna Church, Maude McGovern, Shellie Williams, Sally Hunt, Carolyn Camacho, Alison Dineen, and Patricia Higgs. Lastly, thank you to everyone at Schiffer, most especially our editors Dinah and Jennifer.

Some of the people listed here belonged in multiple categories, and we know, too, that there probably will be someone missing. If it is you, please accept our apologies. We hope you know it is a reflection on us and our spotty record-keeping and not on your value to us. Thank You!

Preface

You may ask how two historians find themselves writing a book of ghost stories. It is because we believe ghost stories are all about history. They, as much as any local legend, newspaper article, or other account, record the history of a place. Ghost stories are an enjoyable way of learning about your community's past. We put this belief into action, first with the Halloween program "In Search of Ghosts" at the Montgomery County Historical Society, and now with this book.

Almost every place has what we think of as universal ghost stories — the stories we all loved listening to during those summer evenings around the campfire. Yet for every one of those ghosts there are so many more that are specific to a community, the results of battles fought and lost, floods and fires, horrific events, politicians who refused to lose an election or are eternally celebrating their win, lovers who never got over the ones who left, work place accidents or train wrecks. The list is endless. In Montgomery County, we can learn about our country's wars, slavery and freedom, farming and industry, commerce and transportation, religion and politics. These are wonderful historical chapters to hear about in and of themselves, but they are so much more compelling when told through the vehicle of a ghost story.

Montgomery County has many ghosts, each with its own story. Some in this book are written by historians and others by the people who experienced the spectral encounter themselves. We invite you to read this book to learn about our county history from a different perspective. We know there are many more stories out there, and we look forward to hearing them. To share your stories go to our Facebook page at www.facebook.com/pages/In-Search-of-Maryland-Ghosts.

REGION I:
PATUXENT WATERSHED

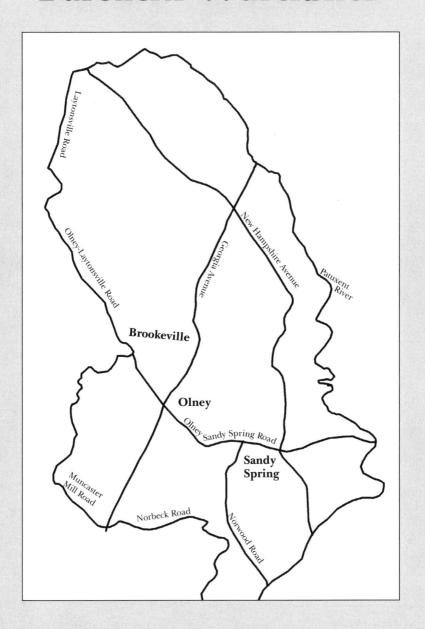

Chapter 1: Brinklow

The Ghost of Old Gold Mine Road

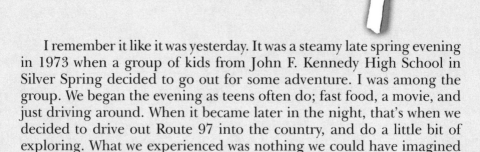

FROM
JEFF PENN

I remember it like it was yesterday. It was a steamy late spring evening in 1973 when a group of kids from John F. Kennedy High School in Silver Spring decided to go out for some adventure. I was among the group. We began the evening as teens often do; fast food, a movie, and just driving around. When it became later in the night, that's when we decided to drive out Route 97 into the country, and do a little bit of exploring. What we experienced was nothing we could have imagined in our wildest dreams.

There were ten of us, packed into two cars as we drove farther out and eventually came upon old Gold Mine Road in Sandy Spring. I remember as we turned our cars onto the road that it didn't look like a normal rural road, but more like something out of an old horror film. At that time, Gold Mine Road was poorly paved, really more of a dirt and gravel road. As we continued our drive, we were surrounded on both sides by large old trees and wooden fences. Perhaps we were in the mood to be spooked, but it looked like the trees were watching us. Their canopies seemed to hang over us like a pair of clasped hands, and grew tighter and closer as we drove. There were no street lights, only the beams of our headlights guiding us as we traveled farther down the road. An old scarecrow greeted us as we rounded a corner, and there, for the first time, we could see houses — old houses. None of them seemed occupied and the darkness and the trees provided an eerie backdrop as we began to pass each one. Suddenly, and without warning, my friend Jeff, who was driving the lead car, stopped. I pulled up behind him and we all got out.

To our immediate left was an old, abandoned house. It looked as if it was built in the early twentieth century, and it was a broken shell of what it once had been. It looked almost as if it had burned in a fire many years earlier. Only gaping holes existed where there were once windows and there was no front door. Inside, from a distance, we could see only blackness, and that's when ten teenagers made a decision that would remain with us for the rest of our lives.

Jeff turned to me and said, "Let's go in and see what we can find." We both pulled our cars around to face the house and used our high beams to light its exterior, so that we could walk through the high grass and weeds toward our unwelcoming host. We began to walk the fifty or so yards through the grass, which became thicker and thicker as we advanced. At times it was almost impassable. When we were around twenty yards from the front door, I heard a scream from one of the girls with us. I looked at her face and immediately saw an expression of shock and horror as she stared toward the structure. I turned back to see what it was that so startled and frightened her, and there it was, framed in the doorway.

At first, I was confused and disoriented. I was now seeing the form of a human standing in the blackness of the opening. The form had no identifiable facial features, but was clearly in the shape of a person. It floated there, without sound, and all became quiet as we were frozen in our tracks. Time seemed to stand still. The apparition was yellowish in color, and took on an almost gaseous appearance. Arms and legs were clearly visible, yet for what seemed like an eternity (but was likely only a second) it made no movement. Then I heard what sounded like a mournful moan, and we all looked at each other and turned to run back toward our cars. It felt as though we were being held in place, as in a dream, while we frantically tried to push farther through the weeds toward our cars without glancing backward toward the house. I yelled out, "Don't stop and talk! Let's just get out of here!" We jumped in our cars and raced out toward the main road, gravel flying as we drove.

When we reached New Hampshire Avenue, we pulled over to the shoulder of the road and got out of our vehicles. We were breathless. As everyone began to shout, I quieted them and asked that rather than influencing each other with our statements, we should write down what we saw and then compare. Jeff pulled a notebook from his car, and we each wrote down what we had witnessed so that we could be sure that we weren't imagining something. As it turned out, all of our recollections were the same.

We left the old Gold Mine Road that night, shaken by what we had seen. We all felt as though we had witnessed some type of paranormal activity at that house, and all believed we had clearly seen what we believed to be a ghost. Whether the apparition was trying to keep us from entering the house or trying to "welcome" us to the home, we'll never know.

The next day, I drove back to the old Gold Mine Road to see in daylight what I had seen the night before, so I could have a better frame of reference. I remembered the entrance to the road. The trees, the fences, the houses — all were familiar. The problem was the house we had all stopped at the night before wasn't there. There was no house. There were our tire tracks and the matted weeds where we had pulled our cars over the night before. There was a clear space where the night before a house had seemingly stood. So I got out of my car and began the walk toward where the house was and discovered, much to my amazement, just a foundation in the ground. The outline of where a house had once stood, perhaps decades before, was just an overgrown stone foundation, blackened by what appeared to be fire or perhaps just age. It was clear to me now. Not only had we seen a ghost the night before, we had seen a "ghost house," the apparition of a building that was no longer there…. I haven't been back since.

Chapter 2: Brookeville

Madison House

BY
KAREN
LOTTES

Heavy footsteps, banging doors, strange breezes — these are typical elements of any haunted house — but what distinguishes the Madison House from so many old houses? Besides being one of the most historic homes in Montgomery County, it has been the site of many odd, inexplicable events. Before exploring the paranormal activity, we should first sketch out the extraordinary significance of this remarkable home.

One of Montgomery County's most famous towns is Brookeville. It is little changed since that day in 1814, August 24th, when Brookeville was a refuge for the Madison administration on its retreat from invading British troops during the War of 1812. Now it is known as the Capital for a Day because of the approximately 36-hour period that President Madison set up his government in exile while he determined the war's next move.

Madison House with the miller's house on the far right.

Near the conclusion of the War of 1812, the British were able to increase their troops and ships in America following the end of the Napoleonic Wars in Europe. Because of this increase in manpower, the British looked at the Chesapeake region and Washington, D.C., the capital of our young republic, as vulnerable to attack. Landing near Benedict, Maryland, on August 19, 1814, the British marched toward Washington. The only things that stood in their way were the guns and seamen commanded by Captain Joshua Barney and the untrained Maryland Militia. Barney had scuttled his fleet near Upper Marlboro to prevent British capture, taking his ship's cannon over land on an arduous journey through the countryside to prevent, or at least slow down, the British advance on Washington. His hope was to give President Madison and his Cabinet time to escape.

The militia standoff came on August 24th at the old dueling grounds in Bladensburg, Prince George's County. The Battle of Bladensburg was an ignoble showing for the Americans. The untrained militia mostly broke and ran. One local hero, George Peter (see "Montanverde," Chapter 10), kept his troops together, hoping to delay the British advance. However, his untrained men were no match for the well-trained veterans of the Napoleonic Wars who continued on, unchecked, to Washington. There, they burned the Capitol and the White House and ransacked the city.

Meanwhile, Madison, who had rushed to the battle scene along with most of his Cabinet, was forced to flee back to Washington and then cross the Potomac to safety in Virginia. His wife, Dolley, had already escaped to Virginia with various White House articles, including that famous portrait of George Washington. After finding Dolley, Madison and his staff crossed back into Maryland, hoping to meet up with his military commander, General Winder, in Rockville, where the troops were to gather and await orders. The question that was uppermost in the minds of the military leadership was which direction the British would go next, north to Baltimore and Ft. McHenry or south to Annapolis. By the time Madison reached Rockville, Winder had moved on, so Madison continued north and spent the night of August 26th in Brookeville, Maryland. This small but prosperous market town of pacifist Quakers was quick to take in the displaced government. Margaret Bayard Smith, who had also traveled north to escape the British, wrote about Brookeville:

> The street of this quiet village, which never before witnessed confusion, is now fill'd with carriages bringing out citizens, baggage wagons, and troops. Mrs. Bentley's house is now crowded, she has been the whole evening sitting at the supper table, giving refreshments to

soldiers and travelers. I suppose every house in the village is equally full. I never saw more benevolent people. "It is against our principles," said she this morning "to have anything to do with war, but we receive and relieve all who come to us." The whole settlement is Quakers.

Madison was given safe haven by Caleb and Henrietta Bentley. Caleb was the Brookeville postmaster and a storeowner. Henrietta was an old friend of Dolley's, both having been raised in the Quaker Society of Friends. The scene at the Bentley's was told to Mrs. Smith:

> ...the scene in B. had been novel and interesting. Just at bed time the Presd. had arrived and all hands went to work to prepare supper and lodgings for him, his companions and guards, – beds were spread in the parlour, the house was filled and guards placed round the house during the night. A large troop of horse likewise arrived and encamp'd for the night, beside the mill-wall in a beautiful little plain, so embosom'd in woods and hills. The tents were scatter'd along the riverlet and the fires they kindled on the ground and the lights within the tents had a beautiful appearance. All the villagers, gentlemen and ladies, young and old, throng'd to see the President. He was tranquil as usual...tho' much distressed by the dreadful event...

At the Bentley home, Madison was able to convene his military advisors and create a plan of action. The determination was that the British would most likely go north to Baltimore, a circumstance that indeed came to pass. It was during the siege of Ft. McHenry, while imprisoned on a British ship in Baltimore Harbor September 13-14, 1814, that Francis Scott Key wrote the "Star-Spangled Banner." This key military engagement led to the British eventually accepting that a war with the Americans was unwinnable.

With a house this historic, is it any wonder that there is a resident ghost? One would think that probably more rather than one spirit would call this place home. The Madison House was built at the beginning of the nineteenth century, around 1804. Fast forward to the twentieth century where ghost stories related to the house endure. When Gene and Juanita Archer saw the Madison House in 1958, they fell in love with it. And they would have had to love it to buy it, because the house had never been modernized — no electricity or plumbing, and the only heat came from the house's many fireplaces. Gene Archer was well-known in Washington, D.C. He was an NBC television personality who also sang the national anthem at many Redskins games and was on the Redskins'

Board of Directors. He left oversight of the renovation to his wife, who lovingly had the house restored and made habitable for a modern family. They lived in the Madison House for thirty years, from 1958 to 1988.

Their long residence at the Madison House meant they had many ghost stories to tell. Heavy clomping footsteps on the stairs, clattering in the attic, and television channels mysteriously changing were regular occurrences. Young Jimmy Archer wrote a story in elementary school about "Johnathan," the name he gave the Madison House ghost. He said that living in a house with four rambunctious boys, a menagerie of pets, and many busy workmen was too much for Johnathan, who, for a time, took refuge in one of the outbuildings. Unfortunately, a tree fell through the roof and Johnathan had to move back into the main house.

The Archers' first introduction to the haunting of Madison House actually came from one of their neighbors. Shortly after they moved in, the couple was invited to a cocktail party. It was during this party that a longtime Brookeville resident said to Mrs. Archer, "You couldn't pay me to stay in that house. Everyone knows it's haunted." However, Mrs. Archer loved the house and was determined to make it their home for a long time. Also on the property was a miller's cottage, which was in equally dilapidated condition. This, too, was restored and, many years later, when the main house was sold, Mrs. Archer kept the miller's cottage for her retirement home.

The Madison House, like many historic homes, had numerous additions and alterations made to it over the years. It had six different levels. With a family of rambunctious boys, you can imagine the house was full of corporeal activity and you would think that might discourage the incorporeal. Not so! One day, the maid was on the third floor working. She heard the attic door slam, but her back was to the door so she couldn't see who might have done the slamming. This was followed by the sounds of footsteps running down two levels of stairs into another room and the slamming of another door. A few minutes later a total reversal of activity occurred with the second door opening and shutting and footsteps going up to the attic, where the door was again opened and slammed shut. The maid had enough and yelled down to Mrs. Archer, "Those boys are home from school and causing a ruckus!" The only problem was the boys were *not* home from school and were certainly not the source of the slamming doors. "You must have an intruder," she yelled down to Mrs. Archer, "and I'm not going to see who." Mrs. Archer grabbed a nine-iron and went to investigate, but, as with most spectral activity, there was no one there.

Jim Archer remembered an event when the kids were all home. It was a snowy day and they were bored. Though not a superstitious family, they had the requisite Ouija board (as many families were wont to have no matter their beliefs) and decided to test it out. Apropos of the setting, they asked if the house was haunted.

"Yes" came the answer.

"Are you a girl or a boy?"

"Girl."

"What is your name?"

"Nancy Helen Riggs."

"What kind of ghost are you?"

"Poltergeist."

Not knowing what a poltergeist was, they called their father at the NBC studio so he could look it up. He told them the definition of a poltergeist was a noisy or mischievous ghost.

They all got a good laugh from the episode. However, later that spring a bunch of them went for a walk near the house. There was some farmland with an abandoned mansion on the property. In the middle of a cornfield nearby was an area that was overgrown with trees and vines. They investigated this area and one of them tripped and landed on a flat stone. It was a gravestone... the gravestone for Nancy Helen Riggs! They had stumbled onto the long neglected Riggs Family Cemetery.

Some years later, Mrs. Archer was home alone in the house. Most of her sons had moved out, and her father-in-law had died, so the rest of the family had gone out of town to the funeral. She invited her friend Teece to spend the night with her. Teece went up to bed early while Mrs. Archer cleaned up for the night. She was staying with Mrs. Archer in the master bedroom. After she had turned out the lights, Teece heard the bedroom door open and close and then the corner of the mattress depressed as if someone had sat on the bed. She turned on the light thinking it was Mrs. Archer coming to bed, but no one was there! As if that wasn't enough, right then before her very eyes, the mattress rose and a few seconds later, the bedroom door opened and shut!

Jim Archer's sister-in-law had problems whenever she visited overnight. She said that someone was continually pulling the covers off her. No one saw it happen or had the same experience. Could their poltergeist, Nancy Helen, have been a little jealous?

One of the scariest events actually took place at the miller's cottage. This was long before Mrs. Archer moved into it. The house had been renovated and was rented out. At the time, the renter was an Episcopal priest who was doing research at Georgetown University about the events on which the story and movie *The Exorcist* was based.

The miller's cottage was a banked building, which means that what is considered the first floor of the building is at ground level in the front and the basement level also opens at ground level in the back (also called a walk-out basement). One day the priest was looking out his window when he saw a woman looking in at him. She wore an old-fashioned, long dress and a bonnet. When she saw he was looking at her, she turned and walked away. Then he realized he was looking out the back window! The woman had been looking in a second story window without a ladder!

After the Archers moved out of the Madison House, no other incidents were reported. The new family was smaller than the Archers (and possibly less rowdy). It's hard to say why, but, for whatever reason, the poltergeist was not as active once they were gone. Maybe she is waiting for a new family to move in who can properly appreciate her tricks!

To read more about the burning of Washington, we suggest *The Burning of Washington: The British Invasion* by Anthony Pitch and *The Battle for Baltimore* by Joseph Whitehorne.

Brookeville Woolen Mill

BY DOROTHY PUGH

Some years back Woody and Kathy Young moved into a charming old stone house set into a hill above Brighton Dam Road. Suddenly one night they were awakened by an overwhelming aroma of lilacs, even though there were no lilac bushes on the property. The strong fragrance just floated through their bedroom. It happened repeatedly, although the Youngs never had lilacs on the property.

The scent just wafted through a room and then disappeared, as if someone were strolling through. Other strange things also happened. Lip prints began appearing on mirrors and windows. Once when the dog's outdoor water dish was dry, it was mysteriously filled, the faucet left running. Sometimes things would disappear from one spot and turn up in another.

Kathy decided they had a ghost — a sweet, considerate spirit that they were happy to have around. Kathy named her Lily Lilac. It seems that when they smelled her fragrance, good things happened. Once when some friends were visiting and discussing a house they were hoping to buy, Lily came whooshing through with her air of lilac and they all felt it was a good omen. It was. The friends got their house almost immediately.

Another time when the house was open for a tour, a woman sensed an "aura." Sure enough, Lily came wandering through and everyone could smell her lilac aroma.

The Youngs' old stone house has been sitting there on its hillside since the late 1700s. It was originally the home of a miller who operated a woolen factory and fulling mill just down the hill in a matching neat, little, stone structure. Both of these buildings are set into the side of the hill, with the house thus acquiring a charming "English basement." Whoever constructed these buildings knew what they were doing. The early rubble masonry work is excellent, and that's probably why these buildings are still standing more than two hundred years later.

This woolen factory used a machine to "card" the coarse fleece fibers by straightening and untangling them with wire brushes attached to rollers. The power source was a water wheel that was turned by a mill race flowing from the Hawlings River.

Brookeville Woolen Mill miller's house and the mill, which is just down hill.

This building was also used as a fulling mill, where people could bring their handmade woolen cloth, loosely woven and full of animal grease, to be made into clean, smooth, felt blankets. Without a mill, the people would have had to finish their cloth the old-fashioned way, having what were probably called "fulling parties," in which they would sit in a circle and stamp their feet on the soap-saturated cloth. Sort of like grape-stomping, only with soap. It might have been great fun, but it didn't do a very good job on the cloth. (The word "fulling" comes from the Old French word "fuler," meaning to tread or walk upon.) In the mill the cloth had to endure a lot more than just what feet could do. It was thoroughly washed in hot water and soap to remove dirt and grease. Then it went into a beating trough with fuller's earth and was "thumped" mechanically for hours. Fuller's earth is absorbent clay, most often of a greenish color. It absorbed most of the natural grease from the wool, but then the fuller's earth itself had to be washed out of the cloth. Quite a process! The wet cloth was stretched on frames, and when dry its top was curried to raise the nap which was then cut down to an even surface. A far superior fabric than what resulted from foot-stomping. Today the finished product would be called "boiled wool," a thick, solid, sometimes even waterproof fabric.

Fulling mills used to be common in the mid-Atlantic in the nineteenth century. They were particularly useful during the embargo period of the War of 1812 when it was difficult to import fabric. These two stone buildings constitute a significant historical complex that seems to be unique in Montgomery County today. This mill is the last remaining fulling mill in the entire area.

There is another, scarier ghost story about this house and mill. An old man who lived there around 1900 said his brother had been murdered in the house. The story goes that his brother had asked a former slave woman to make him a sandwich. For some reason she put ground glass in it and he died. What could possibly have been her motivation to do such a thing? We don't know where in the house he died, but there seems to be something going on in the basement of the miller's house and maybe in the mill itself. Some people just feel something bad in those places. A husky teenager said he would never go back down in the house cellar again, no matter how interesting that "English basement" might be!

Kathy and Woody, though, never felt the bad aura. They were just happy to have Lily kissing windows and gently wafting her lilac scent through the old mill house. An earlier resident had also noticed the lilac smell in his bedroom. Some workers who were renovating the house for him said that his bedroom was where a hired girl used to sleep years before. They said that she always wore very strong lilac perfume…so now we know!

Postscript: The Youngs have moved on and the current owners have never felt any unusual activity in the house. However, they love their historic home and Lily's story, so they have planted many lilac bushes around the property. It just seemed fitting.

Prospect Hill

BY
DOROTHY
PUGH

On a gentle rise looking south over the meandering Hawlings River sits a large, pleasant, old house appropriately named Prospect Hill. It is believed that this house was built sometime after 1750 by John Holland, an English immigrant. His descendants must have liked the place because they occupied it for more than two hundred years. The original land grant was named "Gittings Ha Ha." After you finish giggling, you may be interested in knowing that a "ha ha" was a deep ditch or abrupt change in ground level that marked the boundary of a piece of land. It was often used to define a garden or merely to keep cattle from wandering off the property.

Prospect Hill.

Later in the eighteenth century, John seemed to have been in favor of the rebellion against Great Britain, because the story is that secret meetings were held in the main room of this house. It was a handy place for the locals to get together to support the upcoming American Revolution. This space seems to have had an affinity for rebellions. It once served as a chapel for church members who had pulled away from the teachings of their former church. Later it held the instruments of rebellion when it was a gun and trophy room. Today it is a lovely living room filled with equally lovely antiques.

The second owner of this house was John's son, Charles G. Holland. He was born in 1796, died in 1850, and is buried in the family graveyard up on the hill behind the house. There have been tales of ghosts in this house for many years and it looks like Charlie has been picked to be the haunt. Perhaps he died in the house, maybe in a small upstairs room. One owner was so sure that room was haunted that she boarded up the door so no one could get in or out. (Except maybe Charlie?) When Archie Kendall Shipe and his wife, Julie, bought the house in 1972 and began remodeling and updating it, they broke down the door. They found that the entire room was covered in religious pictures. They were pasted all over the walls and ceiling. Hoping to erase that haunted feeling, the Shipes turned the room into a much-needed bathroom. One can only wonder what Charlie's ghost thought of this change.

The age of the house seemed authenticated by some of the Shipes' discoveries during their renovation. There was an old silver spoon with the Holland family crest on the front and an early eighteenth century English silversmith's mark on the back. There were also early 1800s American coins and a store of antique medicine bottles. The bottles lend credence to the story that the house was used as a hospital after the Battle of Antietam. Or it just may be that Charlie was a hypochondriac.

When the Shipes owned the place, Archie was convinced that "Old Charlie" was still wandering around the plantation and he challenged anyone to visit that dark, mysterious graveyard late at night. According to Archie, "It's always darker up there." Surprisingly, the lovely lady who owns the house today doesn't find it scary. In fact, she had a charming stone bench moved up there so she can sit and relax on a summer day in that little shaded graveyard. She remarked that, "There are very nice people up there." An obelisk listing various deceased Hollands sadly includes two small children, each younger than a year. Of course, "Old Charlie" is named on that small pillar, too, with his grave lying right next to it. It's nice to imagine him stopping his wanderings and sitting down to enjoy that bench on some of those dark, eerie nights.

Greenwood

BY
KAREN
LOTTES

Out Georgia Avenue sits Greenwood, one of the oldest houses in Montgomery County. The original wing, built as a one-room structure, is said to date back to 1723. Like many old homes, it has been added onto over the years as families grew and modernization took place; by 1860 it had grown into a mansion of seventeen rooms.

Greenwood, view from the west, 1936.
Source: HABS, Library of Congress.

Greenwood was the home of the Davis family. Just like the home, the Davis plantation grew from the original land purchase in 1720 of one hundred acres to more than 3,000 acres before the Civil War started in 1861. The original one hundred acres began as a land speculation scheme by Major John Bradford, who only kept it for two years before selling to Richard Snowden. (It's hard to believe that barely settled Montgomery County had land speculators even then!) Snowden built the original one-room home, but quickly sold it to Ephraim Davis, the first Davis. It became known as Greenwood in 1800.

Over the years, the plantation's farming operation grew to include such diverse crops as tobacco, corn, wheat, and fruit trees. Cows, pigs, and sheep were raised. There were grist, cider, and saw mills. A blacksmith shop and an iron foundry were also part of the establishment. All that land and its subsidiary operations were farmed and maintained by nearly one hundred enslaved men and women. Generations of Davis' and their enslaved workers, plus love, devotion, and a little tragedy, make for just the right recipe for a haunted house.

Often we attribute ghosts to the lonely survivors of long-lost love; condemned to restless wandering by their unrequited passion. Other times the love is of a place and the desire to stay in a home that one has lived in their whole life. This appears to be the case with Greenwood and one of its owners, Allen Bowie Davis, and his descendants.

Allen Bowie Davis was born February 16, 1790, at Greenwood and inherited the property upon his father's death in 1833. He enlarged the estate over time so that by the beginning of the Civil War he owned more than 3,000 acres of land, 1,500 of it being the home farm with additional properties throughout Montgomery and Howard counties. With his large slave holdings, he was able to farm the land, managing extensive operations that included crops, dairy, and sheep. He had overseers at each of the different properties. Following the emancipation of all Maryland slaves in 1864 (the Emancipation Proclamation, effective January 1, 1863, did not apply to Maryland as it had not seceded from the Union), Davis sold much of the land and chose to lease the rest to tenant farmers rather than farm it himself as he no longer had the advantage of a cheap labor force.

Allen Bowie Davis loved Greenwood. His wish was to be buried in the family burial plot on the grounds. He is said to have remarked, "Like Rob Roy, the heather that I have trod upon when living must bloom over me when I am dead." So it is understandable that the many sounds of a man walking through the house when all is quiet are attributed to Allen Bowie, still enjoying the home he loved so much.

However, the story doesn't end there. Following Allen Bowie's death, the home farm was sold out of the family in 1906 to David Craver, who was the head caretaker for Davis, and then in 1926 to Wilbur Nash, Sr. Members of the Nash family have reported seeing a woman in the doorway of the hall leading to the Blue Room. The woman was older, with white hair and wearing a blue and white dress with a high collar. She looked very much like she was from the nineteenth century.

Visitors using the Blue Room, part of the 1854 addition, have been frequently woken from their sleep at night by someone shaking one of their shoulders. They have also heard their names being called and chains being rattled. Despite it being a guest room and not in regular use, the bed was always rumpled, like someone had been sleeping in it, despite no one using it once it had been made up. In the 1970s, Melanie and Lynn Nash and two male friends from Baltimore spent the night at Greenwood following a dance that was held near the farm. One of the men wanted to stay in the Blue Room as he had heard it was haunted. Three times during the night his sleep was disturbed by someone tapping him on the shoulder, causing him to wake with a start. The third time he had enough and ran from the room, seeking protection from his friend who was in another part of the house. He never returned to Greenwood.

Who is the woman in the Blue Room? After one of the sightings, family members were looking at old photographs of the house and its former owners. There was a picture of Rebecca Davis, the very image of the specter who makes the Blue Room her home, right down to the style of dress. Allen Bowie wasn't the only Davis who loved Greenwood. His daughters Rebecca and Mary loved the house, too, and had continued to spend summers there after Wilbur Nash, Sr., bought it. Clearly Rebecca loved it as much as Allen Bowie did.

Rebecca Davis,
daughter of Allen
Bowie Davis.
*Courtesy of the
Montgomery County
Historical Society.*

Later owners, Leonard and Betty Becraft, and some friends held a séance one cold night near the Blue Room. They were trying to talk to some of the Nash and Davis ancestors. Suddenly the door shut, the lights flickered, and then the electricity went off for good. Everyone ran from the room only to spend a cold night in other rooms without any heat. Needless to say, no more séances!

We suspect that the last ghost who seems to have loved Greenwood so much he didn't want to leave is Wilbur Nash, Jr. Nash had a distinctive walk due to a limp he had acquired late in life. His very distinctive walk, the footsteps of a person with a limp, continues to be heard in the house. A fourteen-year-old granddaughter said that her dead grandfather, whom she identified by his limp, had covered her up in bed one night when she was cold. What a delight Greenwood must have been for all who lived there, to love it as much in death as they did in life!

However, it can't be said that Greenwood was a wonderful place for all its residents. We can't forget the many enslaved people who lived and toiled there without benefit of free will. It is here that tragedy enters the story, for in the old slave kitchen of Greenwood, there is a tragic presence. Visitors have frequently commented on the feeling of someone or something being present. During the Bicentennial house tour, one visitor kept clutching herself, feeling the cold spirits in the room. Family stories say that Allen Bowie Davis was something of a kindly slave owner. He was not too harsh with his slaves, and when slavery ended in Maryland on November 1, 1864, he took the news well. Reportedly, he called all his slaves to come to the main house so he could talk to them. He read the proclamation ending slavery in Maryland and is then reported to have said, "You are now free men and women. You may go where you wish and do as you please, but unless you behave yourselves, remember what I have taught you, and keep out of trouble, you will come to know a slavery far worse than any you have known under my care."

As the news sunk in, there was quite a scene among his former slaves. Some were shouting for joy, others left immediately, and some went quietly back to work. One of the former slaves, a dairymaid named Charlotte, was overcome by the excitement. She had a stroke that night and died the next day, never to know the true feeling of freedom; her soul still roaming Greenwood, trapped in slavery for eternity. Davis and the now free African Americans were left to bury her in the old Slave Cemetery beyond the barn.

The ghosts of other enslaved men and women haunt Greenwood as well. Some are attributed to an event that took place one Sunday in 1860. Allen Bowie Davis and his wife Hester were attending church at

St. John's Episcopal Church in Olney when he was informed that two of his slaves had stolen a carriage from Greenwood and were heading north on Westminster Pike (Route 97). They were caught in Cooksville and returned to Greenwood, where they were shackled to iron rings in the cellar. Slaves held there were generally sold "down South," a dreaded punishment for Montgomery County slaves. It meant being separated from family and usually put in a place where escape was much harder and living conditions were harsher. To this day, the sounds of rattling chains can be heard in the cellar, the spirits of those two and other shackled slaves.

People aren't the only spirits to haunt Greenwood. Prior to the Civil War, Davis' pet, Newfoundland, was found dead out in a field, having been killed. They never caught the dog's killer, but the pet was buried in the family cemetery. His ghost is said to haunt the fields as he continues to roam. Slaves were often very superstitious and the story of a ghost dog helped to keep them in at night out of fear of what they might encounter.

Finally, Greenwood is home to the only chicken ghost found in Montgomery County. One summer a Leghorn chicken moseyed into the old kitchen and was accidentally closed inside as the house was locked up when the family went away on vacation. No one considered that there might be a loose chicken in the house. The chicken made her way up the stairs, finally finding the attic where she died. For years after she could be heard pecking and scratching on the floors.

Leonard Allen Becraft contributed to this story.

Referred to as the Old Slave Kitchen, this wing includes the oldest part of Greenwood from 1723. Originally a one-story structure, it was later enlarged to two stories. Image is from 1936. *Source: HABS, Library of Congress.*

Chapter 3: Ednor

Clifton

BY KAREN LOTTES

"It takes a heap o'living to make a house a home," wrote Sandy Spring historian, Roger Brooke Farquhar, about Clifton, and he couldn't have been more accurate. Clifton is one of the oldest houses in Montgomery County, dating to the early 1740s, and was home to generations of the Thomas family. A home with that kind of history almost needs to come with its own ghost and Clifton sure doesn't disappoint! Aunt Betsy is the "authentic" ghost of Clifton. She is often heard moaning in the cellar, where there is reported to have been a whipping post. The fact that Aunt Betsy still roams around — slamming doors and blowing out candles — is "vouched for," says Farquhar.

Clifton was built sometime after 1742 by John Thomas, making it one of Montgomery County's oldest standing structures. It is thought that Thomas imported the bricks from England, and architectural historians who have studied the structure believe it could be true. Montgomery County was still very young (and, in fact, was not Montgomery County yet; that happened in 1776) and would not have had the manufacturing capability to make the quality bricks used in Clifton's construction. John and Elizabeth Snowden Thomas had no children, and at his death in 1826 (Elizabeth had died around 1806), John left his property to his great-nephew William Thomas. For six generations Clifton remained in the Thomas family. In 1958, it was bought by Theodore and Frances Wellens; they lived there for ten years. In 1981, it was sold to Dr. and Mrs. James Bullard.

The Thomases that built and owned Clifton were Quakers and one of the founding families of Sandy Spring's Society of Friends Meeting. The Society of Friends was one of the leading advocates of abolition and very early on began to take steps toward eliminating slave ownership among its members. As early as 1778, talk of expulsion of members who continued to be slave owners had begun. In Sandy Spring, all ownership of enslaved people by members of the Society of Friends had ended by 1820. John Thomas clearly believed in the immorality of slavery. By 1800, he no longer had enslaved people living on or working his land, although the census does note free African Americans living at his property.

Clifton in 1936. *Source: HABS, Library of Congress.*

Clifton today.

Therefore, if Aunt Betsy, Clifton's resident ghost, is supposed to have been a slave who went mad, then Clifton has been haunted long before people thought of it as an "old haunted house." Aunt Betsy is supposed to have gone crazy while being kept in the basement where the original "whipping post" is said to have been. It seems unusual for a Quaker like John Thomas, presumably non-violent and anti-slavery, to have kept such a thing, let alone in his home. Could a post like that have some other not quite so nefarious purpose? We may never know, but since Aunt Betsy seems to haunt Clifton from cellar to attic, her restless spirit does not feel as confined as she was in life. Also, even though Aunt Betsy was likely a free woman rather than enslaved, because she was an African American, finding out who she was becomes a tremendous challenge.

As early as 1862 there was mention of Aunt Betsy who may be heard on stormy nights sighing and groaning through the cavernous cellars at Clifton, to the great terror of Uncle Johnny's great-great nieces and nephews, when they went down by candlelight to draw a pitcher of cider or get a basket of apples, recalled resident Sarah Miller. Restless and mischievous, that was Aunt Betsy.

Edith Bentley Thomas came to Clifton as a young bride in 1906. She had many encounters with Aunt Betsy during her time there. Frequently she would hear Aunt Betsy come down the back stairs and see the door open. She also had a reputation of slamming doors when she was upset. The dining room was a particularly favorite spot of hers, perhaps because it had eight doors! On many occasions, when sitting in the dining room, one could see one door open and then an opposing door open and be slammed shut. A much better way to make her point! One of the younger family members remembers hearing a rocking chair in the garret above his room where no one lived and no rocking chair sat.

The cellar door was always opening and would not stay shut — once Aunt Betsy tripped one of the Thomas' on the cellar stairs. That was the final straw for William John Thomas, the last Thomas to live at Clifton. He successfully created an "Aunt Betsy plug" to keep the cellar door shut. It jammed the latch and, apparently, made it too difficult for Betsy to play her usual tricks.

In 1958, the Wellen family bought Clifton. Mrs. Wellen took to Betsy immediately and remembered her as a "happy haunt:" "She gave me a sense of security that was nice. I was never alarmed or frightened because I knew she was there and she was happy and good." Shortly after the Wellens moved in, Mrs. Wellen took a picture of her husband standing in front of the house. It shows an attic window with a missing pane of glass and a white form in the window. When they went to fix the problem, the glass was in place and no one had been in the attic. Also, the dogs would not go in the attic or the cellar.

The Wellens particularly had trouble with one of the barns that stood about one hundred feet from the house. Lights would regularly turn on by themselves. After traipsing out to the barn to turn off the light and then back to the house, they would frequently turn to see the lights back on again! This happened regularly, mostly in the winter of course. Aunt Betsy wouldn't want her antics to be pleasant or convenient! In addition to all this, music could frequently be heard playing softly in the dining room, electric lights went on and off, and the china closet door was constantly opening and closing, the normal haunted happenings.

Aunt Betsy continued in her usual way after the Wellens moved out and the Bullards moved in. Mrs. Bullard also remembers Aunt Betsy giving her a sense of goodness and well being. Certainly no one has ever seemed to mind Aunt Betsy and her antics much. She continues to be one of Montgomery County's best documented ghosts, appearing in newspaper articles and on television shows about historic Montgomery County regularly.

Chapter 4: Olney

Fair Hill I

BY KAREN LOTTES

Sweeping the stairs may sound like a commonplace activity, but in an old, haunted house it can take on new dimensions. Mrs. Lamborne found that out for herself one afternoon at her home in Olney, known as "Fair Hill I." She was sweeping cobwebs off the stairs when a horse and rider rode through the open front door and up the stairs. A horse and rider may not have been an unusual sight in Olney in the 1950s, but one who had the audacity to ride through the house certainly was! Taking her broom she chased them from the house where she saw them ride off and into the ground disappearing at a grave in the small graveyard that was part of the property. Suddenly her courage deserted her as she realized who it was and what might have happened. She had been warned about Colonel Brooke, and now that she had seen him with her own eyes all she could do was scream (a perfectly reasonable reaction)!

Fair Hill I, 1936. This building is no longer standing.
Source: HABS, Library of Congress

Like many old houses, "Fair Hill I" was supposed to be haunted. This grand manor house was built in Olney circa 1770 by Colonel Richard Brooke, a Quaker who served with the Revolutionary army. And, like many old houses, it has a story to tell about the many different roles it played for many different people, along the way collecting a ghost or two to add to the story. Also, as with many an old house, it is no longer standing, having burned down and been replaced by a shopping center.

"Fair Hill I" was once part of a 347-acre farm given to Colonel Richard Brooke by his father, James Brooke, sometime around 1770. Richard Brooke built a large manor house for himself and his wife, Jane Lynn Brooke, when he was only twenty-four. The Brookes were a Quaker family, and it must have been upsetting to James when Richard took a commission in the Revolutionary army. Richard Brooke died in 1788 and was buried in a little plot on the property. And so our first ghost came into being. Accounts of a ghostly Colonel Brooke riding his horse through the house, up one set of stairs and down the other, have been told in Olney from a very early date. Could his Quaker soul, normally used to pacifism, be troubled by his military past? Or is his love for the hunt too strong to desert him in death? In the *Annals of Sandy Spring*, Roger Brooke Farquhar recounts seeing the ghostly Colonel riding to the hounds while he was sitting in a neighboring garden enjoying the afternoon. As the inveterate chronicler of Sandy Spring history, who would know better who the ghostly hunter was than Roger?

The farm was passed down through the family until it was sold, in 1803, to George Frazer Warfield, who turned around and sold it ten days later to George Ellicott (flipping houses is obviously nothing new). Ellicott was a businessman from Baltimore. He bought the property to provide rental housing for the Irish craftsmen imported to work at the pottery factory in Olney. Eight families lived in the house, which must have seen a lot of wear and tear at the time. As a result, a more tragic figure becomes connected to the house — apparently one of these men saw fit to hang himself in the cellar! What could have induced the Irish Catholic potter to commit suicide? We may never know, but clearly his heart was troubled.

In 1817, "Fair Hill I" was sold to Whitson Canby, who turned it over to the Baltimore Yearly Meeting for use as a school. Quakers had a strong belief in the importance of a good education for both men and women. Fair Hill was a large, well situated property even if it was a little dilapidated from its use as a boarding house. It took a couple of years for the Meeting to get the building fixed up, with Fair Hill School opening in 1819 as a co-educational school, headed by Samuel and Anna Thomas, well-known educators. However, within a year and a half, both Thomases had died. Although the school continued on, it never quite recovered from those deaths, and it closed in 1826. The Baltimore Yearly Meeting, which owned the building, tried again in 1851, leasing it to Richard S. and Mary W. Kirk, who established the Fair Hill Boarding School for Girls. The school was well-regarded, but the Kirks suffered a tragic loss when their daughter, Margaret, a precocious five-year-old, died on June 20, 1862, during a local diphtheria epidemic.

Another young, and perhaps more tragic, ghost is that of the baby who was supposed to have burned to death in a fireplace. The child was African American and, while it was unlikely to have been a slave, it may have belonged to a family who worked for Col. Brooke or in the school. While an official account of the child's death has not been found, there have been numerous reports of a baby's wailing heard in the wall behind the fireplace. Since news coverage of Montgomery County was not very complete until after the Civil War, it makes sense that the child died before then.

By all reports, the Kirks were very successful in running the school, but unfortunately the Civil War interfered, and by 1865 the school had closed. The Kirks bought the property from the Baltimore Meeting and ran it as a farm. It eventually was sold out of the family in 1923 when the farm was broken up into building lots. In 1949, the house was sold to the Lamborne family.

Mrs. Lamborne's encounter with Colonel Brooke was very dramatic, but she and her family experienced other haunted happenings at Fair Hill over the years — nothing too alarming, but spooky nonetheless. Little Margaret, who died in 1862, was seen in her nightgown and mobcap sitting at the top of the stairs, and our unknown Irishman appeared to inhabit the cellar. The eerie sound of a baby's cry was heard from time to time. One can only wonder what happened to them after Fair Hill burned down.

Olney House

BY
DOROTHY
PUGH

This large, beautiful home provided Olney with its present name. One story has it that the village was originally named Fair Hill, perhaps after the house that used to stand directly across the road from the Olney House (see the previous story on "Fair Hill I"), and then for a number of years it was called Mechanicsville because it was an artisan's center, the primary business being Whitson Canby's pottery operation. However, when the village fathers petitioned for a post office in 1851, they were informed that there already was a Mechanicsville post office in southern Maryland. They had to come up with another name and so Olney was chosen; perhaps because that lovely old house was so close to the crossroads — or maybe because it was occupied by an old and important family. We are told that Sarah Farquhar, the widow who owned the house at the time, was never happy with the village being named after her home, but Olney it has remained.

Olney House, 1936, now Ricciuti's Restaurant.
Source: HABS, Library of Congress.

Part of Olney House may have been there as early as 1779, occupied by a Mr. Owens who is reported to have lived in the vicinity on a tract named "Shepherd's Hard Fortune." Olney House stands on a section of that original tract. In 1817, the above mentioned Whitson Canby bought the house, but at that time it was still a very small cottage. However, after it came into the hands of Dr. Charles and Sarah Brooke Farquhar in 1840, it grew immensely. They built extensive additions on both ends of the house, dwarfing the original cottage. Charles "signed" the chimney on the left side of the house with metal initials C. F. and the year 1841. Later another addition was added to the house for Dr. Farquhar's mother. The Farquhars named their expansive, comfortable home "Olney" in honor of their favorite poet, William Cowper, who once lived in Olney, Buckinghamshire, England. Members of the Farquhar family lived in this house for almost a hundred years. It continued as a private home until 1974 and then was divided into six, small, upscale shops.

In one of these, the "Touch of Class" beauty salon, strange things started to happen. The curling irons would heat by themselves, hand mirrors refused to stay turned down, and, in the words of co-owner Lisa McKillop, "the lights and doors misbehaved." This was all typical ghostly behavior. Feeling that this surely was a friendly ghost, the other owner, Sharon Damulis, called her Agnes, but later Sharon suddenly fell to the floor and felt that she had been pushed. Guess you need to be careful when naming ghosts.

This haunt also showed up in the bookstore upstairs. There was a lovely little statue of the Virgin Mary standing on a shelf, but every morning when the owner came in, it was turned to face the wall. Could we guess that the spirit didn't like the name Mary either? The only religious connection found was that at one time the building had been leased to the Catholic Diocese as a rectory for the local priests. Perhaps their spirits didn't like a female watching over them.

It's intriguing to imagine that our ghost might have at one time materialized into a cat. One showed up at the shop unexpectedly one day and just made herself at home. They called her Sassy, and she seemed to be alright with that. No one was being pushed around. Sassy even loved to sit in customers' laps. She came and went by herself...and then one day she just went. She never came back. Bye-bye Sassy.

Olney House has kept evolving and changing over the years. Restaurants have occupied it at least twice. In the 1990s, "Olney House Inn" served well-received Italian-type food. By 2000, the restaurant had a new owner, chef, and a new name: "Ricciuti's Brick Oven Pizza." Today it is simply "Ricciuti's Restaurant."

Cognizant of the long history of the building, the owner, James Ricciuti, has retained the name "Olney House" in his sign above the front door. In fact, in renovating the building, one of his workers discovered some very old letters. They seem to be to and from young people discussing their school work and their relatives and friends. One was written November 28, 1846, in Baltimore, from someone named Jeanie to a Miss Maggie Hallowell, Brookeville. The second was written May 7, 1859, to Miss Eliza Farquhar at Fair Hill Boarding School for Girls, just across the street from Olney House. This one was only signed with an initial, either an F or an L. There was also an invitation for Anna Farquhar to a party at Howard Stabler's house on August 21, 1856. The history goes on.

Back to our ghosts, though... In recent times, it seems spooky things have begun to happen again. In the morning, the owner will come in and find the faucets pouring out water. Things will have been moved. One night the alarm went off, police were called, the door was found open, and a police dog tracked someone to the third-floor attic, but as is usual with ghosts, no one was there.

Sounds of a rocking chair can be heard up in that attic. The owner has moved a rocker up there recently, but it cannot be making the noise — it's a glider. We might mention that a former resident, Edith Farquhar, was a lady of "rocking chair age" when she died in this house early in the twentieth century.

A few years ago a child was leaving the restaurant with her mother after having lunch when she looked back and saw a young girl in one of the attic dormer windows. She told her mother, but the mother couldn't see anyone. We understand that there have been other sightings of this young girl, too. This time the spirit was given the name Nancy. She is supposed to be a young girl, ten or twelve years old, who lived there in the early 1800s. She was killed in a hunting accident in a field near the house. Could she have been looking for a playmate when she watched the other little girl leaving?

Nanny

BY DOROTHY PUGH

Quite a few years back when Norma Miller was visiting friends near Olney, a cow escaped from its pasture and had to be rounded up on Route 108, the Olney-Laytonsville Road. It seemed to be a routine happening in that then quiet, four-cornered, rural village. Norma was charmed, and thought it would be the perfect place in which to raise her four young daughters. When the old Samuel White house, sitting at the end of a short road near 108, became available, Norma grabbed it. This house had started life in the early 1800s as a small log cabin, but in the intervening years it had grown considerably and now boasted a covering of solid white clapboards. Still, it had low doors, steep stairs, and walls that were a foot thick. There were 200-year-old trees in the front yard. This place had seen a lot of history.

When the family moved in, they put some boxes in the basement, including one that contained an old non-working clock. That night it awoke them by chiming eleven times! Norma didn't think much of it, but two months later she had a more chilling experience. She was awakened in the middle of the night by her bedroom door opening. Thinking it was a child, she asked what the problem was, but there was no answer, just a low light that she thought might be a flashlight. The door closed, and the light started to glow with a green color. It looked like a grapefruit-sized, mirrored dance hall ball. Norma thought at first that she must be dreaming, but after pinching herself, she knew that she was definitely wide awake. Amazingly, she was not intimidated. She sat up in bed and said, "I don't know who the heck you are, but I pay the mortgage here, and if you want to stay, you had better behave yourself!" Norma felt her house had been invaded. She was more angry than frightened. However, the ball began to grow and gyrate rapidly and turned an angry-looking reddish color, but when it came near a mirror, the reflection must have shocked it because it got smaller and paler and finally disappeared completely. Norma again heard the door open and close.

The Samuel White House as it appeared in 1974.
Source: Montgomery County Historic Preservation Commission.

The ball never showed up again, but strange things began to happen with the lights in the house. One daughter would be awakened every morning at 5 a.m. by all her lights coming on. No explanation was found. When they originally moved in, there had been a burned-out light bulb over the stairs that they couldn't reach. However, at the first thunderstorm when all the rest of the lights went out, this one came on! During another storm, when the entire rest of the neighborhood was black, all of their lights stayed on. There seemed to be a good "light-fairy" watching over them.

Norma and her girls felt that they weren't the only ones living in the house, but Norma never thought of their "visitor" as a ghost — rather that it was a "presence." They actually felt protected and cared for by this presence, so they decided to call her "Nanny." They counted on her because she had been very helpful, especially with the lights. However, during another thunderstorm, when their lights went out, Nanny seemed to be asleep at the switch. One of the daughters tried her flashlight, but it wouldn't work. She stumbled through the dark hall toward the bathroom, when suddenly a glowing figure appeared in the doorway, lighting her way. As she got closer, it faded, but her flashlight came on, providing the necessary light! Nanny was keeping her own schedule!

Nanny played the usual tricks on the family, moving things from place to place, turning radios on, and once letting a daughter hear someone breathing loudly outside her bedroom door when there was no one there. While that one was a little scary, most of the time Nanny really did seem to watch over the family.

One day Norma was taking care of a baby granddaughter. She left the little girl asleep on her tummy in her carriage in a front room, while Norma went to move laundry from the washer to the dryer. The baby started crying, but Norma decided to get all the laundry into the dryer before returning to the front room. When she got back she heard music and was surprised to find the lid open on a previously closed music box. It was turned on, giving out a spritely tune, and the baby was on her back smiling. Protective Nanny was at work again.

When Norma and her daughters moved from the house, they hoped Nanny would come with them. They felt close to her, and they liked her watching over them and taking care of them. The last thing they said in that house was, "Are you coming, Nanny?" Apparently she didn't because, in the new house, there were no green balls, no strange lights, no radios or music boxes turning on by themselves, no feeling of a presence, but still... Often when a daughter was far away and needed her mother, Norma would get a strange feeling and she would call. Sure enough, the daughter needed her. Norma thought it might well have been Nanny making sure that she got the message. She hoped so, anyway.

Postscript: Many years after hearing this story about Nanny, I visited the house and found an empty, abandoned building, completely overgrown with trees, shrubs, and vines. In other words, a very haunted-looking house! A sound caused me to look up, and there in an open attic window perched a huge turkey vulture staring down at me. As I watched, he flew down to a low branch, the better to keep an eye on me. Worried that he might attack, I circled around the house, but the vulture kept following. He never took his beady little eyes off me. Finally, feeling very spooked, I hurried away, wondering why sweet, little, old Nanny wasn't there to protect me. Had Nanny left when the house was abandoned? Or had she moved up into the attic and morphed into that scary, black vulture? Who knows what forms ghosts take?

Olney Theatre

BY DOROTHY PUGH

As Montgomery County grew through the years, so did Olney Theatre. What began as a small summer stock operation on the Olney-Sandy Spring Road back in 1938 has blossomed into a cultural center boasting three separate year-round theaters. These are professional theaters with performances by professional actors. Offerings include twentieth century American plays, premiers of new works, reinterpretations of classics, musical theater, etc. You name it and it has probably appeared at Olney. However, not only are there wonderful shows to be seen, but also the Theatre Center offers a variety of educational opportunities for both young viewers and aspiring young professionals. It's a true blessing for the area.

The local residents don't seem to be the only ones who enjoy Olney Theatre, though. In the wonderful, big, old house that serves as a residence for traveling actors, there have been some very ghostly happenings. This house was built in 1898 by a Quaker couple, Henry and Elizabeth Davis, who christened it Knollton. Both died in the house, Henry in 1904 and Elizabeth in 1925. Elizabeth must have been a very private person because she requested that no memorials of any kind should be written about her. Could she be sorry about that now and be one of the ghosts, trying to make sure that people remember her? Or is she just unhappy that "theater people" are enjoying her lovely, old home? Or are some of these "theater people" the ones doing the cavorting as our ghosts? All we know is that the building is definitely haunted.

Olney Theatre, ca. 1975, the old Knollton Family
House enlarged to accommodate resident actors.
Courtesy Montgomery County Historical Society.

Some years back when the theater was only open in the summer, Bill
Graham, Jr., the managing director, planned to stay in the house for a
few days after the season ended. He was there alone. The first night he
went around and locked all the doors and then went to bed. He awoke
in the middle of the night to the sound of a piano being played. There
were pianos located in the long, wrap-around enclosed porch. As Bill
headed down the hall to investigate, the sound moved from one end
of the porch to the other. By the time he could check the pianos, the
sound had ceased.

He went back upstairs and, as he closed his door, he noticed a smoky,
white substance seeping under the door. It materialized into several faces
which then swirled around his head. He immediately dove into bed,
pulling the covers over his head. When he looked again, they were gone.
Much later, when telling about the faces, he described them as similar to
"Casper the Friendly Ghost" rather than some really scary spooks. Still,
he decided to move out the next day.

The next evening, after loading things into a van, he went back into the house where his girlfriend was waiting for him. She had a shocked look on her face because she was sure she had just seen him going up the stairs. She had heard furniture being moved upstairs, too, but there was no one else in the building! On querying people who had lived in the house at various times, Bill found that many had seen apparitions moving down halls, going up stairs, and even walking right through doors! Always when they were alone in the building — or thought they were alone!

Two months later, Bill was working in his office inside the same building while a big burly plasterer was redoing the ceiling. As night fell, Bill went home, leaving the man to finish. The next day the plasterer stormed into the office screaming obscenities at Bill, insisting that someone else had been in the house and "weird things" had happened. After Bill calmed him down, he agreed to continue the work in the daytime, but never again after dark.

Of course, there were people who did not believe these ghostly stories. One such person was so anxious to disprove the existence of supernatural beings that he asked to sleep in the house the night of New Year's Day, a few months after Bill's scary experience. He fell asleep easily, but awoke suddenly at 3 a.m., feeling all wrapped up like a mummy! He couldn't move or make a sound. He felt a force holding him down. He struggled against it and eventually recovered movement and speech. He was back to his old self, except that he never again questioned the existence of the spirit world.

It's intriguing to wonder who these ghosts might be. There surely are more spirits than Elizabeth Davis here. After all, many dramatic personalities have slept in this old house. It is doubtful that anyone will remember Elissa Landi of "movie fame," who starred in the first production at Olney on July 25, 1938, in Ladislaus Bus-Fekete's "The Lady has a Heart." More recently many other well-known actors have performed here, including even Helen Hayes, long the First Lady of the American Theater. Other famous performers who have trod the boards at Olney are Lillian Gish, Gloria Swanson, John Carradine, Olivia de Havilland, Paulette Goddard, Ian McKellen, Willard Scott, and Roy Scheider. Still other former residents are Carol Channing, Pernell Roberts, Burl Ives, Sam Wannamaker, Chris Sarandon, John McGiver, Olympia Dukakis, and even Nancy Davis Reagan. Jessica Tandy and Hume Cronyn performed their delightful "The Four-Poster" here. Marcia Gay Harden, a star of the television show *Royal Pains*, has played Olney.

So has John Slattery, star of television's *Mad Men*. Another time one of the actors wasn't really an actor, but the Washington Redskins' Hall of Fame running back, John Riggins. In 1992, Riggins played a coach in "Illegal Motion."

In 1949, President and Mrs. Truman attended the American debut of Sarah Churchill (daughter of Sir Winston) in "The Philadelphia Story" at Olney. Unfortunately, there is no record of their reaction to Sarah's work. Other presidential families have also been entertained at this state theater of Maryland.

A sad story connected to the theater involves Mary MacArthur, the well-loved daughter of Helen Hayes and her husband, the playwright Charles MacArthur. In the summer of 1948, the nineteen-year-old girl was appearing at the Olney Theatre in preparation for her Broadway debut. She became ill and soon died of an infection, possibly polio. It was a very traumatic experience for all concerned, and perhaps Mary's ghost is still there trying to finish her performance.

Fortunately, most of those housed in the actors' residence over the years have had a happier time of it. One actress who performed in more than twenty plays there likened it to a pleasant summer camp. She stressed the serenity, saying that it had a "really nice feel to it." She thought living together in that large, old house was "special" and that it brought the actors closer to each other, creating a "family atmosphere." Perhaps that's why the ghosts love this place; they feel like members of the "family," too.

In the early years, the actor residents were expected to pitch in with the household chores. Some of them enjoyed it and even cooked. Jose Ferrer was famous for his paella, which he served to everyone. Others helped by picking fruit from the trees on the grounds and making pies, jam, and other goodies. Certainly, this was a nice break from acting.

At one time Olney had a pool that the actors could use for cooling off when they weren't performing. Definitely a good thing since in the beginning the theater wasn't air conditioned. The walls did have big shutters that could be opened for air flow when necessary. So it wasn't surprising when a dog walked onto the stage one night in the middle of a play! A less pleasant experience for the audience was when a black snake dropped down from a rafter. Going to the theater in Olney could be exciting!

Another famous actress who played at Olney was Tallulah Bankhead, who appeared in "Private Lives" in 1949. Her father, William B. Bankhead, served in the U.S. Congress and was Speaker of the House for many years, so you would think Tallulah would be quite dignified, even with that wild name. Au contraire! After staying at the residence a few days, she was asked to leave because she was keeping the others awake half the night with her boisterous and unruly antics. She was moved into a small stone structure that had originally been built as a gas station. She didn't seem to mind, even planting roses in front of it. But she may also have been planning for ghostly appearances in years to come, because there is a story that one night she was sleepwalking and wandered out onto the highway, stopping traffic. There were some very surprised travelers because Tallulah never bothered with a nightgown or pajamas! It is suspected that now her ghost may have moved from the gas station back into Room 3 in the residence, as many weird sounds have emanated from there, and figures have been seen walking through the closed door. Tallulah may be hanging around, still enjoying herself at Olney.

This little house became Tallulah Bankhead's home during the run of "Private Lives" after she had worn out her welcome at the actors' residence.

Chapter 5: Sandy Spring

Boo and Bloomfield

BY KAREN LOTTES

There is a house in Sandy Spring where children are happy to go to bed. What is this magical place? Bloomfield!

Bloomfield was built before 1806 by a Quaker, Richard Thomas. Caleb and Henrietta Thomas Bentley were given the 100-acre property, Bloomfield, by Henrietta's family and were in residence there by 1818. Previously, when they lived in Brookeville, their home was what is known today as the "Madison House," the home where President Madison took refuge when he was fleeing the British in 1814 during the War of 1812 (see "Madison House" in Chapter 2). After their move to Sandy Spring, the Bentleys opened a general store. Caleb's son Richard was the first Bentley to really consider Bloomfield home, and he made many changes to the house. Richard was very active in the life of Sandy Spring and was one of its leading citizens.

Bloomfield was originally a three-story house with five bedrooms on the second floor and two on the third. There were full porches on the front and rear of the house. In the years since the Bentleys first moved in, much remodeling has occurred to the building. Columns have been added to the front of the house to give it a more colonial look and additions have enlarged it. In 1914, Bloomfield was sold out of the family.

As Quakers, the Bentleys did not own slaves. In addition, local tradition makes the home a stop on the Underground Railroad. There is no evidence it was used to house runaway slaves, but stories do say that the Bentleys aided slaves on their way north with supplies and directions. There are a number of families in the Sandy Spring area that have been connected with the Underground Railroad because of the political sentiments of the abolitionist Quakers.

Boo's home, Bloomfield, 1999.
Source: Montgomery County Historic Preservation Commission.

Traditionally, the two rooms on the third floor of Bloomfield have
served as the nursery. It is in this home that generations of Bentleys and
their relations, as well as the families that came after them, have grown
up — and it is here that the resident ghost lives.

In the 1970s, the Patterson family bought Bloomfield. They found their
son, Groves, was happy to go to bed. He had an "invisible friend" whom
he called Boo — a young boy with long blond hair and he wore a long
nightshirt that looked like it was made out of a feed sack. Boo played with
Groves' toys every night and helped make bedtime fun. The Pattersons
thought nothing of this. Many children have imaginary friends and, as
this one seemed to make bedtime easier, who were they to complain.

A curious thing happened, though. When the children of house
guests stayed on the third floor, they often had the same story to tell.
The descriptions were always the same — a young boy with long blond
hair and a long nightshirt that looked like a feed sack, though sometimes
the children called the apparition "Aah" instead of Boo. "Boo" never
appeared to adults and those children who had played with him said he
stopped appearing once they became teenagers.

Once, an elderly woman on a house tour asked to see the third floor rooms. She said she had spent summers at Bloomfield as a child. The most curious thing, though, was that she wanted to know about her childhood playmate... Was Boo still around? The young boy with long blonde hair and a nightshirt like a feed sack?

Auburn

BY DOROTHY PUGH

Sometimes people just cannot bear to leave their beloved homes and property. Lucy and Joseph Stabler must be such people. They lived their whole lives in their familiar, comfortable home, Auburn, just down the road from the Sandy Spring Meeting House. Auburn was constructed as a story-and-a-half home in 1818, a year after the Meeting House was built. It's probable that both buildings were constructed of bricks from a large, clay pit then located just across the Olney-Sandy Spring Road. Members of the Stabler family and their descendants lived at Auburn for more than a century, during which time it grew considerably, becoming a spacious family home. Lucy and Joseph were two of the six children of William Henry and Eliza Thomas Stabler, the first owners of Auburn. Three of these children — Lucy, Joseph, and Ellen — never married and continued to live in the family home for many years.

As a child, Joseph tended the livestock in the fields, there being no fences. He was often seen walking the acreage. In later years, after the property was enclosed and Joseph was the owner, he still kept an eye on the fields. It had become a deeply ingrained habit. So ingrained, in fact, that people say that in recent years they've seen his ghost still out there patrolling the property. It's no wonder as Joseph was a great lover of nature who, to quote volume IV of *The Annals of Sandy Spring*, spent his time "putting his strength and heart into the farm that was to him as almost a living personality." He continued working his farm nearly up to his death in 1915 when he was close to eighty-eight years of age.

Although he was beloved by friends who knew of his kindness and generosity, he did present a stern and austere appearance to the outside world — and that was the face the Sherwood School students saw in the 1880s and 1890s when their athletic field backed up to Auburn's fields. Roger Brooke Farquhar states in *Old Homes and History of Montgomery County, Maryland* that Joseph was no minor terror when a stray football or baseball landed in some of his bountiful crops of wheat or corn and had to be retrieved by a young scamp of a schoolboy. Many such balls were left where they fell until 'Cousin Joe' had passed out of sight and hearing. According to people who have seen his ghost, he's still guarding against errant balls that might damage his property.

Auburn, Joseph and Lucy Stabler's home.

Sisters Ellen and Lucy Stabler lived with their brother Joseph at Auburn. They were also said to have austere visages, Ellen being known as a stern school teacher. However, Lucy, despite a forbidding look, was said to have a generous nature and to always be ready to practice charitable giving. Lucy died at Auburn in 1897 while Ellen ended her days at a niece's home in 1924.

Lucy seems to be the other ghost at Auburn. Some years after both Joseph and Lucy were gone, a four-year-old boy named David was staying at the house. One day he announced to his mother, "I saw the pointy lady last night." He described her as a very little lady, wearing a cap and carrying a slender cane. She had come into his room during the night, making no noise and saying nothing. She just pointed her cane at him. Although she visited him several more times, she never spoke a word, just pointed the cane. His description of her matched "Aunt" Lucy Stabler. It seems that Lucy and Joseph, who never left Auburn in life, also can't bear to leave it in death.

The present owners have not been lucky enough to see Joseph or Lucy or any other active spirits, but they have named their brother and sister dogs "Joe" and "Lucy" as a neat protective measure.

NORTHERN COUNTY

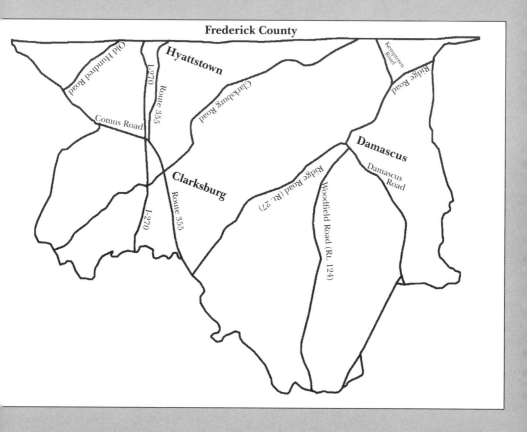

Chapter 6: Clarksburg

Little Bennett Regional Park

BY DOROTHY PUGH

Strange things used to go on in Little Bennett Regional Park's Nature Center building back in the 1980s. The wooden stairs from the basement would suddenly creak and groan as if someone was walking up them when actually no one was. Although this is not unusual, especially in a place peopled with ghosts, this noise was bad enough that a carpenter was called in to make sure the stairs were safe. He could find nothing wrong with them, but the noise continued. It would suddenly start and then stop just as suddenly, especially when someone was alone in the building.

The noise was more continuous when park employee Denise Gibbs would be alone and playing music. At that time, the noise on the stairs was constant, slowly driving her crazy. Luckily she discovered that country music would calm this spirit and stop the stair activity. This spirit must have liked Denise because it seems to have even traveled with her. Once, while driving to Germantown, she was listening to popular music on the radio. When she arrived at her destination, she parked, turned the motor off, got out, and locked the car. When she returned to the car, the radio station had been changed. You guessed it — it was now playing country music!

Heavy drapes covered the windows at the Nature Center and they were always pulled shut at night. The first person to arrive each morning would often see part of a drape pulled to the side as if someone was looking out. Many people noticed this.

The lobby of the building contained ten country-style twig rockers. When someone sat in one and rocked, the floor would complain and emit typical squeaks and scrapes. This was fine when someone was in a rocker, but this noise arose periodically when the rockers were unoccupied. Members of the staff would look and just see empty rockers rocking away while the floor voiced its protest. Again a carpenter was called in, this time to check the floor, both the boards on the top and in the basement. But once again all was fine.

Late one day after Denise and fellow staff member, John Baines, had led long, tiring hikes, they went to rest in two of the rockers. John sat down first. But when Denise tried to lower herself onto the seat of the second rocker, she felt that something was already there. It was very strange. Then she felt a push and was forced back upright. Some unseen person was already sitting in her chair, and he or she had just pushed Denise out of it!

The weirdest thing of all happened when the building wasn't going to be used anymore. Denise and John were packing up to move out, and Denise was sitting at one end of her eight-foot-long desk. High on a shelf on the wall behind her was a large set of deer antlers. John Baines was in the next room with the door open. He saw those antlers come down off the wall right above Denise's head, hover a while, and then slide through the air the whole length of that desk and then crash to the floor and roll away. Both John and Denise saw it. They couldn't imagine deer antlers rolling, but that set did.

On her very last day in the building, Denise went down to the basement to lock up the three sets of double doors that were down there. She bolted them and headed back up the stairs. At the first landing, she stopped and looked back. The doors were all open! As she watched, they opened and closed many times. Denise could sense anger in the air. Someone didn't want to be locked in or out.

Denise felt there were really two ghosts in the building: a mischievous male spook who had pushed her out of the rocker and a female who peeked out the window each morning. Whoever they were, they really enjoyed surprising Denise and John.

When that building was reopened later, Denise was offered an office in it. She immediately said, "No!" She had had enough of those playful spirits. No more!

In searching for possible reasons that ghosts inhabited that building, we discovered that it had formerly been a church. Denise was told that two people had died there; one was a natural death while the other was the result of foul play. Unfortunately, this could not be confirmed. With the closing of this former religious building, the ghosts seem to have decamped.

Postscript: These days the building, now known as Hawk's Reach Activity Center, is once again open in the summer. Little Bennett Regional Park could actually accommodate plenty of spirits if they wished to return, as it is the largest park in the Maryland-National Capital Park and Planning Commission system with 3,700 acres. Activities in the park include camping, hiking, cycling, horseback riding, and birding. Interpretive programs are given periodically, art shows appear at the old Hyattstown Mill, and there is even a golf course. Add to this the fourteen known historic sites within the park, and it is clear there is plenty of room for the ghosts to continue to frolic.

Chapter 7: Goshen

The Ghosts of Honeysuckle Hill

BY KAREN LOTTES

In Goshen there stands a house that dates to 1820 called "Honeysuckle Hill." Built by John and Anne (Smith Waters) Jones, the house stayed in the family until 1929. It is a largish home that "slips sideways down the steep hill," as Katherine Riggs Poole remembered it. It was originally on three levels with the kitchen raised on stilts in order to be level with the dining room. In Miss Poole's youth, the house was well furnished with an eclectic assortment of pieces as befits a family house decked out in the Victorian manner. The shutters were kept closed in summer to keep the heat down and opened during winter days to let the sun warm the rooms.

Following the death of the last Jones descendant, Emma Jones Riggs, the house was sold out of the family and eventually fell into disrepair. In the 1960s, the house was renovated and sold. The new owners soon learned the secret of Honeysuckle Hill. For this rather imposing house, formerly home to many Montgomery Countians representing well-known family names such as Linthicum, Riggs, Waters, and Poole, is haunted. It has regular seasonal visitors that come every April and November to the home they knew, and still know, so well.

In November, a bleak month to be sure, the new owners met their first spirit. The female owner heard a loud thumping noise as if something was falling down the stairs. But when she went to investigate, nothing was there. No one else was home at the time, and the family pets were behaving very oddly. The dog was running up and down the stairs barking madly, and the cat's hair was raised and it was hissing furiously.

Her family dismissed the experience until one night her husband felt someone shake him awake — only no one was there. The incidents happened again. Finally she saw an apparition of a young, white woman in the attic. When November ended, so did the hauntings…simply to return the following November.

After some investigation, the owners decided the ghost must be that of Annie P. Linthicum. Her gravestone, which stands in the family cemetery on the property, is set apart from the other stones, all of which are for Jones family members. The gravestone reads:

Honeysuckle Hill. Today, the house is greatly enlarged from the original home.

"Annie P. Linthicum
died November 24, 1869 aged 26
Though he slay me, yet, will I trust in him."

Annie was the daughter of Mary Ellen Jones (John and Anne Jones' daughter) and Lloyd Linthicum. There is a family legend that she hanged herself in the attic. Very little is known of her or what her reason was for ending her life in such a drastic fashion. She is clearly reliving the past as she re-visits Honeysuckle Hill every November.

The second ghost appeared in the spring. April is a month of rebirth, not one people usually associate with hauntings. Shortly after the month began the owners heard voices. They were of a young woman crying and begging a man not to leave her. He was clearly trying to comfort her.

Headstone for Annie Linthicum from the family cemetery on the grounds of Honeysuckle Hill.

Though the voices were difficult to understand, the gist of the conversation was recognizable. Again the animals went crazy and behaved in bizarre ways. This same scene was heard throughout the month.

After some research, the new ghosts were identified as Emma Jones Riggs, who was the last Jones to live in the house, and Washington Griffith, her fiancé. "Wash," as she affectionately called him, was a clerk at Riggs Bank and destined to go far. However, when he was only twenty-one years old, he contracted a fatal illness and died. Emma begged her family to let her marry Wash on his deathbed, but they refused. He died in April. After his death, she wore the wide band he had intended for her wedding ring until her death. She had his hair made into a brooch and earrings that she also wore until her death, the only other jewelry she owned.

When Emma was in her sixties, she married Reuben Riggs, although the marriage in no way diminished her devotion to Wash. His portrait continued to hang over her bed until her death, and Reuben's ring was placed above Wash's on her finger. Emma also died in April, in the year 1929. Apparently her ghost is reluctant to leave the place she called home for so many years.

Old Goshen Church

BY
DOROTHY
PUGH

One of the strangest ghosts in Montgomery County was seen in front of the old Goshen Mennonite Church on Brink Road. It was right at sunset in the late 1980s. A horse trainer was driving home from her job in Etchison that evening when she found her eyes mysteriously drawn to the old church. It seemed to be exuding a green glow. When she pulled her eyes back to the road she had to slam on her brakes because there was a man standing in front of her with his hands outstretched to stop her! He was dressed all in black with a broad-brimmed hat on his head. When the woman looked at his face, she was shocked to see it was a skull! His hands were just skinny bones! It was a skeleton dressed up to look like a minister. Her car couldn't stop in time, and she braced for the hit, but the car kept on going. She couldn't see the man anymore, so she looked in her rearview mirror, and there he was stopping the car behind her. She had driven right through him! She heard the brakes squeal on the other car, but she didn't wait to find out what happened. She hit the accelerator and headed for home as fast as she could.

Old Goshen Mennonite Church. This is the third church structure that has stood on this property.

Soon she began having recurring dreams of an oak leaf. It had its own intriguing style, which puzzled her so she drew a picture of it. A friend suggested that it might be connected to that mysterious old church where she had seen the skeleton, so she visited it with her picture. She found a large oak tree there, but its leaves were different. Wandering through the adjoining cemetery, she happened upon a tombstone with the name "Waters," and what to her wondering eye should appear but her very own oak leaf. There it was!

Many members of the Waters family had belonged to this church from its very beginning, and quite a few of them are buried in this graveyard. The oak turns up again in the name of the home of one Zacharia Maccubbin Waters, the Younger: It's Oakhurst, right there in Goshen. However, this Zacharia isn't buried at Old Goshen, but you can find the tombstone of his father, Zacharia Maccubbin Waters, the Elder, there.

The old church goes back to before 1790. A group of Methodists had built a little log church, called the "Goshen Meeting House" (aka "Goshen Preaching House"), there. Ignacious Pigman gave them a deed to the one-acre it stood on for five shillings. Pigman, a very religious man, served as the first Methodist circuit rider in Montgomery County. He was also a large land owner and is credited with building an early mill on Goshen Branch. It was probably only fitting that after Pigman's generous donation, the church became known as "Pigman's Chapel." Later it was called "Goshen Chapel," even later "Goshen Methodist Church," and finally it officially became "Goshen Methodist Episcopal Church."

This first Methodist church in the county was very plain with just plank benches for seating. However, the minister had a reasonably tall pulpit. When he sat down behind it, the congregation could not see him. There is a story that as members came into the church on one Sunday morning they were laughing and talking when a sepulchral voice, seemingly out of nowhere, admonished them with the words, "The Lord is in His Holy Temple, let all the earth keep silence before Him."

This little log church served the congregation well for more than forty years. It was even used as a school. Richard Waters, Jr., better known as "Uncle Dicky," taught there for many years. It has also been reported that Bishop Asbury visited in its early days. One of its strongest and most active ministers was James Paynter, who helped the congregation build a nice, new, brick church in 1830. A brick kiln was constructed in the field across the street to provide the building materials. These homemade bricks formed the new church which rose on the site of the old log one. It had three doors, one for the ladies, one for the gentlemen, and one leading to the rear gallery for the slaves. Within the church a low partition divided the men's and women's sides.

The Reverend James Paynter, who loved the church he had helped build, wanted to be buried at the back of the pulpit, and so he was when he died on March 1, 1840. However, the cracked slab we can now see marking his grave is quite a few feet in FRONT of the present (third) church, very close to the road. Is it possible the foundations of Rev. Paynter's church are under the present road? The location of his grave seems to indicate this.

By 1869, the second church building was feeling its years and it was unsafe to use, so once again the congregation built a new church, probably a little distance behind the old one. However, parts of the old church carried over, as they were able to reuse some of those old bricks made in the kiln across the road. The old chandelier also made it into the new church. It hangs in the back with a newer one in the front. This new church is of an unusual design. It has a high Mansard roof covered with fish scale shingles, and instead of a steeple there is a tall arch projecting from the center front of the church. This protects a well-defined rose window of clear glass displaying eight petals around the center.

Eventually, the Goshen Methodist congregation merged with Laytonsville Methodist and they chose the Laytonsville church as their new home. There were no more Methodist services in the Old Goshen Church, but in 1950, the building was leased to the Eastern Mennonite Board of Missions and Charities for use by their organization. They have made many improvements, and services continue to be held in the old church.

Remember the skeleton in the road that scared that woman driving home past the old church? Well, about ten years later on a dark and foggy night another woman was also driving home past that same church. According to her, there was a real pea-soup fog, so she slowed down because visibility was almost nil, but she did manage to see the man who stepped right in front of her car and held his hand up, signaling her to stop or at least slow down. He was dressed in old-fashioned clothing, wearing a coat with big buttons and a hat. He had a beard and she thought he was a full-bodied man — certainly not a skeleton — but even going slowly, she couldn't stop in time and passed right through him, just like the previous driver who had driven through the skeleton. When she asked around in the neighborhood, she learned that others had also passed through that same man in the road. Still others remembered passing through a skeleton.

You would think two ghosts in the same place would be enough, but yet another ghostly being has been spotted on that same stretch of road — a black dog with red eyes. He's been seen by many people. In fact, they named him "Plucky Lucky."

Are these human ghosts manifestations of old Preacher James Paynter as he tries to keep people from driving through his church? Did he have a pet dog named Lucky? In matching black? What's the connection with the Waters' and the oak leaves? Could it be Uncle Dicky? We'll probably never know, but keep your eyes peeled when driving past that Old Goshen Church.

Bloodstain on the Floor

BY DOROTHY PUGH

Something went on during the Civil War in an old farmhouse in the Goshen area. We don't know what, but a soldier was killed. We don't even know which army he belonged to, but we do know that as he died, his blood spilled out onto the floor. It left a stain which refused to be removed. During the middle of the twentieth century, the resident family tried and tried to remove the stain. After they worked on it, they would think they had eliminated it only to have it return again. It even floated up to discolor their rug! Another stain that refused to be removed. This soldier really wanted to be remembered!

He may have stayed because of an attachment to a family member or servant who had a small room near the landing of the front staircase. One cold and snowy night the owners of the house invited a guest to stay because of the terrible weather. She was given that small servant's room near the landing. This room was unusually chilly, but the guest was just glad to crawl under the covers and go to sleep. Unfortunately, she didn't get much sleep because those covers kept slipping off the bed onto the floor. She would wake up shivering and pull them back up, only to lose them again as soon as she went to sleep. Upon complaining to her hosts in the morning, they apologized and told her that they suspected there was a ghost in that room. They thought it was a whimsical, prankster-type ghost, and it seems they were right! Have the soldier and maid joined forces to entertain and amuse the residents of that particular room?

Chapter 8: Laytonsville

The Plum Creek Poltergeist

BY DOROTHY PUGH

A house doesn't have to be old to have ghosts. When this house on Plum Creek Drive was only three years old, the owners experienced many strange things. They may have been super-sensitive because they said they could feel spirits cavorting around the house for days at a time. Evidently the ghosts would leave for a while and then return for another round. Their manifestations seemed centered on the master bedroom where they would periodically make the lights flash on and off. When they tired of that, they would become visible as an illuminated "chunk" of fog hanging right there above the bed, according to the owners.

When that disappeared and the owners were able to get to sleep, they would often be awakened later by sounds of water plop, plop, plopping. Perhaps the fog was melting...but that wouldn't explain the sound of booming kettledrums at the same time? These were really weird spirits.

As might be expected, it became difficult to find babysitters to stay there at night. At least one refused to return, saying that among other strange things, objects would fly around the room. The Plum Creek Poltergeist showing its true colors? Or not, since no one else ever saw anything except the fog, and it was almost colorless.

These sensitive owners have moved on, and we think the poltergeist or poltergeists went with them as things are pretty calm in the Plum Creek area these days.

Layton House

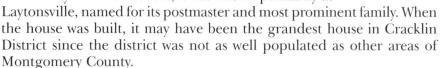

BY
KAREN
LOTTES

The Layton House is a Federal-style brick home built circa 1800, most likely by Uriah Layton. When the house was built, Laytonsville still went by its original name of Cracklintown, as it was part of the Cracklin District. By the 1850 census, it was known primarily as Laytonsville, named for its postmaster and most prominent family. When the house was built, it may have been the grandest house in Cracklin District since the district was not as well populated as other areas of Montgomery County.

Let us skip ahead a few generations and owners. By the 1970s the house and its outbuildings contained several antique stores and they were known to be haunted. The store owners said they couldn't keep doors locked, and they frequently smelled the aroma of baking beans. They also found it difficult to keep small collectibles, particularly marbles, in stock as they were always disappearing. On two separate occasions a ghost hunter (paranormal psychic) came to the house. Each of them sensed a friendly spirit, but it was indistinct.

Layton House, 1936.
Source: HABS, Library of Congress.

On one occasion, the renter of an upstairs room, who had a five-year-old son, heard her child talking to someone. When she went to see who it was, she found him sitting by the fireplace holding a conversation with someone she couldn't see. When she asked him who he was talking to, he said, "Don't you see the boy next to me?" When she asked the boy's name, her son didn't know what it was. Old-timers from Laytonsville had heard of a mulatto child, the illegitimate child of the enslaved cook and one of the white owners, who was supposedly kept in the attic. That could also have accounted for the smell of baked beans that was found in the attic.

There was also a malevolent presence at the top of the cellar steps sensed by several visitors with psychic abilities. (Not the ones previously mentioned, who only sensed friendly spirits. Evidently many psychics visited this "haunted house.") One of the stories told about the house tells of an enslaved man who was chained in the cellar because of his behavior. He managed to escape his shackles only to be shot and killed when he reached the top of the stairs. Where this story originated is unknown and it has not been documented. However, the killing of a seemingly dangerous slave was not necessarily newsworthy in antebellum Montgomery County and could have easily gone unrecorded.

In 1979, the Wilkinson family rescued the Layton House from possible demolition. They had fallen in love with the property, but it had been badly neglected over the years and needed a great deal of restoration work. As work started on the house, the family began to experience the quirks of living in a haunted house. One day Tom Wilkinson was working alone in the house on the second floor landing above the front entrance. The front door had been replaced with a temporary door which could lock. He was working on repairing the windows and window sashes when he heard the temporary door open and footsteps going through the hall and starting up the stairs. When he looked over the balcony, there was no one there. When he went downstairs, he found the front door locked.

On the third floor, where that little boy had been playing with his "imaginary friend," the Wilkinsons had rooms for an au pair. All the au pairs felt the presence of a little girl. When they first moved in, there was strange activity with lights going on and off and doors opening and closing unexpectedly. After a bit, however, the activity stopped, probably after the ghost got used to its new roommate.

Finally, all those marbles that had disappeared from the antiques stores? They began re-appearing when the Wilkinsons renovated Layton House. They were found throughout the house, in the ceilings, under the floorboards, in the clocks, even outside in the dirt.

Since the restoration, the only spirit anyone has sensed is the girl on the third floor. Perhaps changing inhabitants and restoration work has scared the other ghosts away, and they have abandoned Layton House completely, even to their cherished marbles.

Chapter 9: Poolesville

Bernie's Club

BY DOROTHY PUGH

More than half a century ago, Bernard N. Siegel, a retired grocery store executive who loved golf, acquired many acres of land south of Poolesville. He called his property Norbern Farms, and he had a grandiose dream of building a satellite community of 30,000 to 40,000 people, complete with all amenities including a splendid golf course. Unfortunately for Bernie, his housing development never got off the ground, but he did get his golf course. Although Bernie hired professionals to design it, he had his way with some things; he insisted on wider greens so duffers such as he was could say they got on the green in regulation. He wanted happy golfers at his course. He wanted beauty, too, so he dammed up Horsepen Branch to create a fourteen-acre lake right in the middle. He called his course River Road Country Club, and the Siegel's original private home became the clubhouse. Bernie loved to walk his course wearing his cowboy boots and his modified ten-gallon western hat.

This lodge at the Potomac Valley Golf Course was originally Bernie's home, which he developed into a clubhouse for the country club.

The club was the highlight of Bernie's life, but by 1966, six years after the opening, Bernie was suffering from serious heart trouble. It must have been more than he could handle because he took his own life that year. The club went on for a while as the renamed Potomac Valley Country Club. Still later the Montgomery County Revenue Authority took it over, but wanted only the golf course. For some years the clubhouse was occupied by an independent catering company, the Potomac Valley Lodge. This is no longer in operation. If you go out there today, you will find the Poolesville Public Golf Course and the large, abandoned, forlorn building that once was Bernie's home and then his clubhouse. It's very sad.

Bernie may be gone, but many who knew him think his very active spirit didn't really leave his beloved course. While the clubhouse was still in use, he could be heard going up and down stairs, walking around whistling, and seen coming through locked doors. His shadow was noticed going down a hall. Twice a white ghostly figure was seen, once in the basement and another time outside. Recently he has been observed at an upstairs window. Some of Bernie's buddies once experienced him yelling at them to go home because he thought they were lingering too long after hours. They obeyed. Bernie wanted people to know that he was still in charge.

At closing time, the clubhouse lights would be turned off. As is typical with haunted buildings, after it was locked up, they often came back on. The television set was included in the fun, seemingly turning on and off at will. In desperation an electrician was called in, and of course everything was fine. Ghosts love to fool around with electricity, but Bernie seemed to want light in his clubhouse, no matter how it was supplied. Even the red candles on the tables would re-light by themselves after being put out for the night. Thank goodness there was never a fire!

One scary episode took place when the lone bartender, a D.C. policeman by day, stepped close to the bar to tend to a customer, then whirled around and demanded, "Who was that? Who walked behind me? Who touched me?" The customers saw nothing but the bartender and didn't know what he was talking about. However, this experienced policeman definitely sensed someone behind him and had felt the person brush by him. There was no one there, so it's not surprising that the bartender said he felt the hairs on his neck rise up.

Another time there was a customer listening to his friends telling some of the Bernie ghost stories. This particular fellow definitely didn't believe in ghosts. He was pooh-poohing everything the others said, so someone suggested he go downstairs and walk through the empty, dark kitchen by himself. He gladly accepted the challenge. A short time later he came back upstairs, yelling, "Who came down here? Who did this? You're trying to fool me! You're not funny!" Yet all the people in the group upstairs had remained in their seats.

The kitchen was being remodeled, and the fellow said that when he got downstairs there was enough light that he could see that one of a double set of doors had been propped open with a five gallon bucket of paint. Suddenly the bucket moved, and the door closed all by itself. He didn't waste any time getting back upstairs. He may have wanted to believe that it was a trick, but he found that none of his friends there that night would venture below stairs. They knew enough not to go down there in the dark.

Sue Demory, a long-time manager of Potomac Valley Lodge, knows all of these stories and has experienced a lot of them herself. She was often alone while closing the place up at night. She knew Bernie's spirit was somewhere around, and she worked as fast as she could just to get out of there. She and two friends were once the last ones in the club. They were just sitting around talking quietly. There was no background music; the jukebox was off. Unexpectedly that jukebox turned itself on and started playing, "Some Fools Never Learn!" Those three women made such a mad dash for the stairs heading outside that they literally fell all over each other trying to get out. Luckily no one was hurt. They just wanted to get out of there fast!

Bernie must have loved parties because once when Sue was working alone at night she heard sounds of talking, laughing, music, and utensils rattling in the empty Gold Room. All sounds of a really great party. She headed for the room to see what was going on. But just as she got to the door, silence descended, and when she opened the door, it was completely dark inside. Another time, a bartender, also alone in the building, had the identical experience that Sue had. Guess Bernie wanted his parties kept private.

Even the restroom wasn't exempt from all these goings-on. Sue entered it one day when she was sure it was empty, but there was whistling coming from one of the stalls! Then there was the time she went in with another employee, and they noticed a name written on the wall. They read it aloud, and the lights started flashing on and off. It was so weird that they said the name again, and the lights became like strobes. It was confusing until they remembered that this was a person whom Bernie really didn't like. Another time a shower turned on by itself, but the most exciting thing was when all the toilets flushed in unison!

It may sound as though Bernie was some kind of scary spook, but in general the people who experienced his tricks seemed to feel that he really was a benevolent soul. They thought he was just a prankster and that he was fun to have around. At least that's what they say now. Your best chance of seeing Bernie is at night when a groundskeeper tours the course with a pickup truck checking on things. You might see Bernie riding along on the tailgate wearing his boots and almost-ten-gallon hat, keeping an eye on HIS club.

1785 House

BY KAREN LOTTES

Sitting in Poolesville on the main road is the puzzlingly named "1785 House." Built circa 1830, this charming house once boasted a separate log cabin kitchen which, if it was still standing, may have explained the misnomer. The 1785 House actually was built in two sections: the oldest, a two-story brick home with an attic, has two rooms on each floor while the second section was built sometime after as a separate townhouse. Eventually they acquired connecting doors. As neither side of the house is particularly large, this chain of events might account for this little house having five first-floor exterior doors, an average of more than one per room.

The 1785 House seems to be haunted by a lonely ghost. The current owner used to rent the second floor of the home out. When it was not rented, there would be the sounds of doors opening and closing and footsteps between rooms. When it was rented, there was no paranormal activity evident. In recent years, he opened up the house so there are no more barriers between floors. Since then, all unaccounted-for activity has stopped. And in a creaky old house, that is something!

Who could our lonely ghost have been? Or were there two, possibly the spinster Jones sisters, Airy Ann and Columbia, who once owned the houses and may have been responsible for connecting the two sides. Perhaps these unmarried ladies are happier now that the divisions have been removed and they can wander the house unencumbered by unexpected walls.

1785 House and close-up of "1785" on side of house
although the house was actually built around 1830.

The Nessul House

BY DOROTHY PUGH

It's a good thing this is a large house, because it seems to contain multitudinous ghosts. One of them is known as The Gray Lady. She first appeared to owner Henry Nessul's mother, who lived with the Nessuls in her later years. She was confined to bed in her last months, and Henry and his wife, Linda, would hear her talking to someone. When asked who it was, Henry's mother replied that she didn't know, but it was "The Gray Lady" and she was "waiting." The Gray Lady never talked, she would just stand at the foot of the bed, and after a while she would float — as if the standing hurt her feet! After Henry's mother died, the Nessuls thought that The Gray Lady may have been standing watch, waiting for Mom to cross over to the other side.

In trying to put a name to the Gray Lady, the Poole family might be considered. Various members owned this house from 1850 until 1903.

Nessul House. Today it is listed as the John Hall House on the National Register of Historic Places.

A Rebecca Poole, who had owned the house earlier, died at her home in Poolesville in 1880. We don't know just where that home was, but she no longer owned this house. The next owners were William Wallace and Avilda Poole. Avilda died in 1894, but again ownership had changed before that date. The new owner was James Frank Poole.

We also have the sad story of Sarah Jones Poole. A widow, she married the also widowed William Wallace Poole, previously married to Avilda. (Both are mentioned above.) The wedding took place April 28, 1899, but instead of long and happy years together, they had only three weeks as William Wallace died suddenly May 26, 1899. Although none of the Poole women mentioned above owned the house when they died, two may have still been living there, and one of them might be the Gray Lady. Or perhaps one of the Poole ladies missed her old home so much that she decided to come back after death.

In Henry's mother's last days she had a caretaker at the house. During this time, Linda's mother had a heart attack, and Linda and Henry needed to stay at the hospital with her. The caretaker was to stay in the house that night. She went into the bedroom she was to use and flipped the light switch. Nothing happened. (She didn't know it, but that switch only controlled the ceiling fan.) She walked into the dark room and complained, "Gee, it would be nice if the lights were on." Immediately they came on! The caretaker was so frightened that she fled the room and found somewhere else to sleep. When Henry and Linda came home in the morning, the lights were still on.

Henry's mother had owned a cat that came to live with them the same time she did. After Mother and the cat were both gone, Linda heard the cat walk into the Great Room, then caught a glimpse of his tail as he crept behind the couch just as he used to. This house has four-legged ghosts, too!

Once, friends came and stayed overnight. They closed their bedroom door. There were no pets in the room. The woman awoke and found a cat on the bed and there was an old woman walking in the room. The friend felt immobilized. She couldn't move, but then she heard a voice say, "It's OK. We won't bother them now." The lady picked up the cat and left. The Nessuls feel this might have been Henry's mother just keeping tabs on things.

Another time when work was being done in the attic of the house, two workmen arrived earlier than a third. They decided to scare him by hiding and moaning and rattling chains. They succeeded. The third man was very frightened, but when the first two came out and laughed about the joke, the third man said that he had also seen a gray lady who disappeared when the first two showed themselves.

Linda's father also came to live with them in his last days. (These Nessuls are wonderful, giving people; taking such good care of their aging parents.) Dad used to see a ghostly young boy and girl who never talked. A three-year-old girl, Margaret Rebekah Hall, died in this house in 1912. The poor child seemed to have kidney problems and had always been frail, but she was a sweet little girl, and the first line of her obituary read, "God needed one more flower in the garden of Heaven, and He called a little child." Unfortunately, no definitive information could be found of any boy dying in the house.

Shortly before Linda's father died, he also noticed young men in uniform standing outside his window. They seemed to be waiting, just as the Gray Lady had been. When Henry and Linda asked what kind of uniforms they were wearing, he replied that they were sailor suits. Linda's father had been in the U.S. Navy in WWII, and he had seen that bloody fighting on Guadalcanal. Perhaps these were long-gone buddies of his who didn't make it home from the battle. Linda's father was never frightened of the spirits he saw; their appearance seemed very natural to him. When he died soon after, the Nessuls thought the sailors might have been waiting for him to join them.

One time an aunt was visiting, and she had lain down to take a nap. Before she closed her eyes, she was looking at the wall in front of her, when it just melted away! She saw the road outside, but it wasn't the modern roads of today — it was an old-fashioned dirt road and a boy was playing in it. Somehow the aunt knew he was named Elias. She saw Elias looking up the road when a milk wagon came from the other way and ran over him! The vision disappeared, and the wall was back. It has been reported that an "Elias" once lived in this house. Perhaps he's the boy who appears with the little girl.

One day when Linda was upstairs, she suddenly noticed a strong, old-fashioned, sweet, floral fragrance. It was so strange that she called Henry to come upstairs without telling him why. When he entered the room he asked her what she had sprayed in the room. They both smelled it. After a while it disappeared — as if someone with strong perfume had left the room. The Gray Lady?

The Nessuls used to own a dog named Paddington that loved cat food. After Paddington had passed on, Linda and Henry were in the kitchen one day where there was a can of cat food on the counter with a lid tightly attached. Suddenly the lid popped off and landed on the floor. Linda and Henry looked at each other and said, "Paddington's back!"

The most recent manifestation of a ghost was in 2011. A roofer came to the house to work on it. He knocked, but there was no answer. Lights were on, so he looked in the window of the Great Room and saw a strange-looking, elderly lady whom he didn't know. She didn't look as though she was going to answer the door. It was dinnertime and the roofer knew the Nessuls sometimes ate at Bassetts, the corner restaurant a few doors away, so he went there and found Henry. However, Henry knew of no elderly lady at his house. They hurried there and could see no one. Henry went in and let the dog out of his cage. The dog walked out and then stopped abruptly, transfixed. Henry looked in the direction of the dog's stare and noticed curtains moving, although the window behind them was closed. Thinking this was one of their spirits, Henry asked it to speak, but as soon as he did, the curtains stopped moving — and the dog started moving. Once again the canine was comfortable.

Maybe it's not so strange to have so many ghosts in and around this house. It's been there awhile, having been built as a log house back in 1804 by Raphael Melton, a Poolesville tailor. Raphael evidently was an entrepreneur because he also had a musket pad in the basement, which was used to make bullets. Molten lead was poured into small hollows in the pad and allowed to harden.

This interesting old house also had some hidden treasures. When renovations were done some years ago, three Confederate cavalry sabers were found behind a wall, all wrapped in newspapers. Back in the Civil War, although Poolesville was in a Union state, most of its populace sympathized with the Confederates.

More renovations uncovered a big stone fireplace in the basement of the log part of the house. It was probably originally used for cooking. A jug was found in it, still containing some foul-smelling liquid. Maybe early corn squeezin's?

Linda and Henry say that these days it is mostly other people who experience ghostly happenings in their house. Since they have been there more than twenty years, the ghosts are probably so used to the family that they don't get any fun out of surprising them anymore. In this house normal and paranormal people all seem to live together very happily.

The Battle of Ball's Bluff

BY
DOROTHY
PUGH

Ball's Bluff rises one hundred feet above the Potomac River on the Virginia side just opposite the 400-acre Harrison's Island. It is south of White's Ferry and a mere two miles east of Leesburg, Virginia. Its main claim to fame is that it was the site of an early battle of the Civil War and now holds the third smallest military cemetery in the country, with just twenty-five gravestones arranged in a circle around the American flag containing fifty-four bodies. However, only one stone has a name on it — James Allen of the 15th Massachusetts Infantry.

National Cemetery at Ball's Bluff.

This battle should never have happened. In the summer of 1861, the Union forces had a "corps of observation" along the Potomac River in Maryland to keep an eye on the Confederates on the other side in Virginia. On October 20, a Union patrol mistakenly reported an unguarded Confederate camp near Ball's Bluff.

It was decided to send a force across the river to investigate. The officer in charge was to be fifty-year-old Colonel Edward D. Baker, who was also a senator from Oregon.

Years earlier Baker had spent time as a lawyer in Illinois, where he and Abraham Lincoln had worked together politically. They became such good friends that the Lincolns named their second son, Edward Baker Lincoln, after Ned Baker. Unfortunately, poor little Eddie died at age four.

When Lincoln took office, Baker rode in the carriage with him up Pennsylvania Avenue to the Capitol. Col. Baker had the honor of introducing Abraham Lincoln for his inaugural address to the people.

In October of 1861, Col. Baker's 71st Pennsylvania Infantry Regiment, also known as the 1st California, was camped in Maryland near Great Falls (see "Great Falls Tavern" and "The Tommyknocker" in Chapter 17). Baker was staying at the Dick Collins farm, and the day before the battle he made a surprising statement to Mrs. Collins, "I have a premonition of death. I never expect to see you folks again."

Baker then rode on down to the White House, where he lounged on the lawn while Lincoln sat leaning against a tree; ten-year-old Willie Lincoln was playing nearby. After discussing the war and the upcoming action, Baker got up to leave. He shook hands with Lincoln, hugged Willie, and was given a bouquet of flowers by Mary Lincoln. Baker looked at her and remarked quietly, "Very beautiful. These flowers and my memory will wither together." He then jumped on his horse and headed up to Poolesville, Maryland, to dine at Annington, a large, impressive house that sits on a hill not far from the Potomac (see "Annington" in Chapter 11).

The next day, October 21, Col. Baker was told to take a Union force to Harrison's Island and then cross over the remainder of the Potomac and climb the one-hundred-foot bluff on the Virginia side in search of the Rebels. It was to be a diversionary tactic, a mere skirmish. If he found a strong Confederate force, he was to retreat. He had general orders from his commanding officer, General Charles Stone, who was located south of the action at Edward's Ferry, but decisions on the ground were Baker's. From the start nothing went right. There weren't enough boats, the cavalry disappeared, units weren't where they were thought to be, officers didn't follow through on orders, communications weren't the best, and Baker himself was late getting to the battle. When he finally arrived on top of the bluff, when it might have been wiser to call for a retreat, he charged ahead in front of his men. He ignored good advice from a subordinate. Although he had fought in the Black Hawk War in Illinois and exhibited unusual bravery in the Mexican War, on this fatal day his military decisions were poor. Kim Bernard Holein, in his book *Battle at Ball's Bluff*, wrote, "Though a man of unquestioned bravery, Baker's tactical decisions reveal his lack of military expertise."

The Union men were mostly in the open while the Confederates had found shelter behind hills, trees, and boulders. The Union forces were pretty much trapped with their backs against the top of the bluff, but Baker strode in front of his men, cautioning them to "lie down" or "lie close." One soldier called out, "But you don't lie close." Baker replied proudly, "When you are a United States Senator, you will not lie down either." Baker's bravado would be his undoing, as a group of Confederate soldiers dashed out of the woods and a big red-headed Rebel with a revolver took aim right at him and fired at least four bullets straight into him. Baker died instantly. The Confederate soldiers rushed over and tried to get Baker's sword, but his men rallied and killed the red-headed Reb and sent the others fleeing. Baker's men managed to get his body down the bluff and onto a boat to Harrison's Island, but his loss demoralized his men and they scrambled rapidly down the cliff and into the water for safety with the Confederates steadily firing down on them. The river was the only escape, but unfortunately the Potomac was swollen with flood waters, some men couldn't swim, and most were heavily laden with clothing and equipment. Many drowned, and bodies washed up all along the shore from Great Falls to Georgetown with some even turning up as far south as Fort Washington, Maryland, about fifty miles south of Balls Bluff. Many agreed with the participant who called the melee "that cursed [Battle of] Balls Bluff."

A Southern sympathizer, Matthew Fields, editor of the *Montgomery County Sentinel*, reported that so many Union soldiers fell into the Potomac during the Battle that fish later caught in the river tasted terrible, like "dead Yankees!"

There was much confusion in trying to get the wounded and the dead bodies back to Maryland. The battle had taken all day, with Baker being killed about five o'clock in the afternoon. His body was first taken to his headquarters, the Frederick Poole House in Poolesville, carried by a group of soldiers that included his nephew, Lt. Edward Jerome, who had also been in the battle. Later, Col. Baker's body was taken on down to Washington. He was the only sitting member of Congress to die in the Civil War.

Lincoln was at Gen. McClellan's headquarters in Washington when he learned of Baker's death. He said nothing, just put both hands to his breast as tears escaped down his cheeks, and he stumbled and almost fell on his way out into the street. One of his oldest and closest friends was gone. Young Willie Lincoln was so moved that he wrote a poem, which was published in the *National Republican*: (Sadly, Willie died of typhoid fever just four months after Colonel Baker, on February 20, 1862.)

> There was no patriot like Baker,
> So noble and so true;
> He fell as a soldier on the field
> His face to the sky of blue…
> No squeamish notions filled his breast,
> The Union was his theme,
> 'No surrender and no compromise,'
> His day thought and night's dream
> His country has her part to play,
> To'rds those he left behind
> His widow and his children—
> She must always keep in mind.

In Washington, Lincoln wanted the body of his good friend, Ned, laid out in the East Room, but Mary Lincoln was in the midst of redecorating and said it couldn't be done. Instead, he was sent to an undertaker on Pennsylvania Avenue while Congress spent days eulogizing him. Services for Col. Baker were at the home of James Wilson Webb at the corner of 14th and F Streets. Mary Lincoln attended wearing a lilac outfit, for which she was roundly criticized by the other ladies of Washington because she didn't wear black. The lengthy funeral cortege to Congressional Cemetery included President Lincoln, Vice President Hannibal Hamlin, all cabinet members, all Supreme Court Justices, and many members of Congress.

Poor Col. Baker was not fated to rest in peace, though. The people of Oregon wanted their senator's body returned to them, but so did California, where he had once been a very active politician with a golden voice. It was claimed that Baker was instrumental in Lincoln's election because he had brought in the West Coast for Lincoln. In the body battle California won out, and Baker was exhumed and put on a train with stops for viewing along the way. When he arrived in California, there was a service and then interment at Lone Mountain Cemetery (later renamed Laurel Hill) where he lay in peace in a large grassy plot on top of the hill, his grave surmounted by a marble incised table. Some eighty years later when development encroached on the cemetery, it was closed, and Col. Baker, his wife, and a son were moved to the San Francisco National Cemetery located in the old Presidio Military Base there. In recent years this base also closed, and it became possible that Col. Baker would have to be dug up and moved again! However, in October 1994 the National Park Service took over the property and left the cemetery intact. It is now part of the large Golden Gate National Recreation Area, in which Fort Baker and Baker Beach commemorate the Colonel. His name also appears on other forts, a street in San Francisco, and a city and a county in Oregon.

With such a wealth of final resting places, it is an honor that Baker has chosen to haunt Annington in Montgomery County, the site of his last dinner. However, there are plenty of spirits haunting the Bluff, the river, and Harrison's Island. They are the poor souls who drowned or were shot while trying to escape their last, most ill-planned battle. You can hear and see them on dark nights still trying to cross the Potomac to safety. Others rise up from that small cemetery on the bluff.

To read more about the Battle of Ball's Bluff, we suggest *Battle at Ball's Bluff* by Kim Bernard Holien and *Ball's Bluff, A Small Battle and Its Long Shadow* by Byron Farwell.

Postscript: A young Lieutenant Oliver Wendell Holmes, Jr., future Chief Justice of the United States Supreme Court, was at Ball's Bluff, too. He was very seriously wounded in the battle, being shot in the chest. He later described the sensation: "I felt as if a horse had kicked me and [I] went over." He nearly died. Luckily he survived, and that's probably why his ghost isn't wandering around the area, too. But his poor body really took a beating in that war as he was wounded twice more before it was over, at Antietam and at Chancellorsville.

Discovering the bodies of the slain in the Potomac River following the Battle of Ball's Bluff. Drawing by Alfred R. Waud, 1861.
Source: Library of Congress.

James Trundle Farm

BY KAREN LOTTES

Along Old River Road, on a promontory that once overlooked the Potomac River, sits a house that towers over visitors as they approach. Perhaps it is because of how proudly it sits on the land, but one gets the sense that if these walls could talk, they would have a lot to say. Surrounding the house are barns, corrals, pastures, equipment, and the other paraphernalia one would expect to see at a horse farm — and always, the wind is blowing, raising up the dust, whipping your hair around, and providing an even greater sense of the past. One might expect the wind to blow out the cobwebs of a place, keep it fresh and bright. Unfortunately, instead, it seems to get into the corners and crevices and swirl the history of this place out into the open, keeping the souls of those who have lived and died here alive. It is the Old James Trundle Farm, now known as Huntview, and it has a long history of ghostly happenings that go back more than sixty years.

James Trundle Farm.

The land that the farmhouse stands on was settled early in the eighteenth century. The current house was built around 1876 by James Trundle. It was not the first house on the property and is said to have been built on the foundations of an older building. Just when ghosts began to trouble the home's residents is hard to say, but it may have started quite early in the twentieth century. The disembodied crying of babies has been reported by most of the residents as well as moaning and footsteps where there are no people around to account for it.

One night sometime during the 1940s, there was a terrible snowstorm. Everything around was shut down and no one was out who didn't have to be. It was evening and the caretaker at the time was looking out the window when he saw footprints in the snow. He called the family together because he had told everyone to stay inside. This was the kind of storm where one could be in great danger outside, but everyone was indoors and no one had gone out. The next morning, the man went out to see what damage the storm might have caused. Under the window where he had seen footprints the previous night, there was a set of deep tracks leading down toward Old River Road. As he followed the tracks, they became shallower and shallower until they disappeared altogether in the middle of a field.

The farmhouse is built in two sections with the old section in the back having a kitchen on the first floor and a bedroom above. In the 1950s, the caretaker at that time was getting very frustrated with the room above the kitchen. He could not keep the door shut. The door had a good latch; yet, it never stayed shut. Every night he latched it when he went to bed and in the morning it had opened. Finally, out of frustration, he decided to sleep in front of the door thinking that his body would prove to be an immovable force. Perhaps he was thinking if he could keep it shut just one night, it might break the cycle. He laid out his sleeping bag and went to sleep right at the door. In the morning he woke up only to find himself halfway down the hall and the door open! Sometimes, ghosts just have to have their own way, and there is nothing you can do about it. The caretaker gave up after that and just let the door do what it wanted.

In addition, the ghosts of Civil War soldiers have been seen with some regularity on the farm. Generally only women see these ghosts. When new equipment is purchased for the farm, ghostly farmers and men in uniform can be seen walking around and inspecting the new machinery, much as they might have done in life.

In the 1960s, the wife of the farm's blacksmith and her sister had gone into the barn to saddle horses for a ride. The sister saw a man in the tack room, and she thought it must be the blacksmith working, and then he was gone without saying hello or responding to her in any way. When she asked him about it later in the day, he said he hadn't been there. In trying to figure out who it could have been, she described a man dressed in what sounded a little like an old-fashioned uniform, much like a soldier from the Civil War.

This horse stall was formerly the tack room where the ghost of a Civil War soldier was seen.

During the Civil War, there were many Union encampments in the Poolesville area and around the Trundle Farm. The ease with which troops could cross the Potomac River near Poolesville, coupled with western Montgomery County's southern sympathies, made it strategically important to have Union troops stationed there. There were a number of news reports of skirmishes and military activity in the area in the early years of the Civil War. There are some accounts that the farmhouse on whose foundations Huntview was built was used as a hospital during that time. While no clear evidence has been found to substantiate this, it is in all likelihood true. The armies of both the North and the South traveled with units of regimental surgeons and other medical staff. During and after major battles, however, the armies hired and commissioned local doctors to help with the wounded. Those commissions of medical personnel usually lasted only a few months. In this way, the army could commission doctors where they needed them and, when the army moved on, taking with them their regimental surgeons, the local doctors would care for the wounded soldiers until they could be moved to the Army's regional general hospitals in and near the cities. There was a Union Army temporary general hospital at the courthouse in Rockville in 1862. When soldiers there became ambulatory, they were moved to one of the several large military hospitals in or near Washington, D.C., for recovery and long term care. One of those hospitals was at St. Elizabeth's in Washington, D.C., near Uniontown (Anacostia).

The current residents believe that perhaps not all the soldiers that should have moved on have done so. They have had many encounters and unexplained happenings since they moved into the farmhouse. Carlos and Adriana felt the house had a heaviness when they moved in, but thought it might have had more to do with how rundown the place was than anything else. They began to have problems almost immediately, first with their daughter's room. As they were fixing the place up, room by room, their daughter was sharing their bedroom. Regularly Adriana would wake up in the early hours of the morning to find her daughter coming into the room crying from elsewhere in the house, as if someone had woken her up and taken her out of the room. Adriana stayed up one night to find out what her daughter was doing. She heard a woman walking in front of her daughter's room groaning.

One evening she left her daughter sleeping in her room as she had to go out. It was dark outside, and the light was on in the bedroom. After she had gone out, Adriana looked up and saw a man in the window by her daughter's bed. On going back upstairs, she found no one there except her sleeping daughter. When she asked her husband who had been there, he said no one, and he had been on the phone, so hadn't been upstairs either. Once, when she fell asleep on her daughter's bed, someone touched her back in the early morning to wake her up. Again, no one was around.

In addition, the sounds of whistling and footsteps, plus doors opening and closing, happen regularly. The moans of a man (or men) on the third floor have woken them up many times. Perhaps the soldiers who died of their wounds in that place have had difficulty accepting their deaths. Loud and vigorous prayer has seemed to help that situation. Something more disturbing happened recently when Adriana fell down the stairs, sustaining very serious injuries. Her footing seemed sound to her and yet she lost her balance… Perhaps an incorporeal push? Such malevolence is out of keeping with all that has happened in the past, but to feel safe she is doing a lot more praying for the troubled souls that seem to haunt the place. Things have gotten better, so possibly Adriana's prayers are proving to be what was needed all along to bring harmony back to the old house.

Chapter 10: Seneca

Montanverde

BY
KAREN
LOTTES

One of the great manor houses of Montgomery County is located in Seneca on Berryville Road. "Montanverde" was built circa 1810 by Major George Peter of the Peter family of Georgetown. The son of Robert Peter, first mayor of Georgetown, George grew up in a wealthy and influential family. The Peter family, while being prominent in its own right, was related through marriage to most of the well-known families in the region including the Custis and Lee families. This tall, distinguished man founded a political empire in Montgomery County and is said not to have let death stand in his way. The sounds of breaking glass and moving furniture, the apparition of a man dressed in riding clothes, and other distinctive paranormal activity all help to attribute Montanverde's ghost to Major Peter.

Montanverde, home of Major George Peter, ca. 1950.
Courtesy Montgomery County Historical Society.

George Peter grew up in Georgetown. At fifteen years old, he ran away from home to join the army. His plan to fight in the Whiskey Rebellion of 1794 was hindered by his parents, who wrote to a family friend, George Washington, to ask for his return. Washington ordered him sent home, but must have maintained a fondness for Peter because, in 1799, he awarded him a commission as a second lieutenant in the army. Peter served with distinction, but he resigned in 1809, following the death of his father. By the time of his resignation, he had achieved the rank of major, had been part of the trial of Aaron Burr, and had organized the first light artillery in the American army. He then began his second career as landed gentry and Maryland politician.

Upon inheriting land in Seneca from his father, Peter purchased an additional five hundred acres from General Montanverde, an officer on the staff of Marquis de Lafayette. George Washington, who himself had owned land in the area and had surveyed it extensively, recommended that Peter begin quarrying the red Seneca sandstone that was found on his property. Sandstone from the Seneca quarries was eventually used in many of the government buildings in Washington, D.C., including the Smithsonian Castle. It was also used to frame the C & O Canal. Peter continued to live in Georgetown, but built the stately Montanverde as his summer home.

Portrait of George Peter.
Courtesy William Offutt.

In 1813, he re-enlisted in the army to help fight in the War of 1812. At the Battle of Bladensburg in August 1814, his troops were the only ones to stand firm in front of the advancing British (see "Madison House," Chapter 2). His achievement that day helped the inexperienced American troops escape the British. It also helped him emerge as one of the few heroes of the Battle for Washington, a status that helped his political ambitions. In 1815, he ran for and won his first political office — as Congressman from Maryland's 6th Congressional District.

In 1937, the Harman family bought the house to use as a summer home. Not long after, they heard the sound of breaking glass and went to investigate. There was nothing there. "I was upstairs fussing about in the rooms," Mrs. Harman recalled, "when I heard the distinct sound of glass shattering. I called to Frank who was downstairs to ask him what it was. He didn't know either. Maybe an ashtray had fallen off a table or a bird had broken a window. We checked and checked and found nothing. No glass. Nothing." This happened regularly and they didn't know what to make of it until someone in town asked if the Major was still up to his old tricks. "Does the old Major still throw his toast glasses into the fireplace?" he asked. And so the sound of the breaking glass was explained.

George Peter was married three times and had fathered sixteen children. As a politician, his home was full of friends, family, and well-known guests. He was fond of a nightly hot toddy and was known to have thrown his empty glass into the fireplace when there was something to celebrate. It is this tradition more than any other occurrence that identifies Montanverde's ghost as Major Peter. To this day breaking glass can frequently be heard as Major Peter celebrates another victory.

In 1948, the Harmans reported hearing great carrying-on and the sounds of a tremendous number of glasses breaking, more than the usual noise. That year of 1948 also happened to be the 100th anniversary of the election of Zachary Taylor, a victory that George Peter helped orchestrate.

Another time the Harmans had done some redecorating and rearranging of the furniture. They were outside working on the grounds when they heard the sounds of moving furniture in the house and went to investigate. They discovered that a comfortable old easy chair had been moved next to the fireplace from a different location in the living room. As they were all out in the yard and there were no visitors, no one but the Major could have moved the chair. It was now located in the best place to enjoy an evening toddy by the fire.

In addition, the sight of a stately gentleman dressed in riding clothes of the nineteenth century can sometimes be seen in the east bedroom. His room in life as it is in death.

Not all of Montanverde's residents have had such a complacent attitude toward the paranormal activity. When Diana Valanidis rented the house, she said that the caretaker had warned her that she wouldn't like it: "There's snakes in the cellar and ghosts upstairs." For the time she lived there, unpleasant ghostly happenings were regularly experienced.

Doors were heard opening and closing, making her dogs howl, something they never did otherwise. She also heard loud noises of drawers opening and closing. Cool breezes went through the house now and then when she couldn't account for them.

A guest of hers had a terrible experience of waking up and seeing someone sitting on her bed — the presence was pressing on her stomach and brushing against her face! She swung her fist — it felt like pushing through warm, fuzzy Jell-O! Really scary! The next night she found everything from her dressing table on the floor, her clock smashed. Another time the room was turned upside-down with a lamp smashed. The sound of loud stomping, as of riding boots, through the house was heard on numerous occasions. Candle flames would first sputter and then get exceptionally tall.

Another person awoke to see a woman with long hair in an old-fashioned long, white dress with a cord tied around the waist. Not only could she see her, but she also could see *through* her! "Almost like the wind was blowing, but there was no wind."

This was such a different experience than the Harmans! To whom can we attribute these other apparitions? Who was the malicious presence? Unfortunately, historical records do not tell us what former resident could be restlessly wandering through the house. The Harmans never felt threatened by any presence and, in fact, they enjoyed having the Major as a permanent guest in his old home. "Who could have anything but a warm feeling for a man who comes back to take a drink?" Mr. Harman said, "Now I sometimes throw my own glass just to be in character!"

Chapter 11: White's Ferry

Annington

BY
DOROTHY
PUGH

High on a hill a mile east of the Potomac on White's Ferry Road sits Annington, a magnificent, brick, three-part Georgian mansion. Its setting not only commands beautiful views of the Maryland countryside, but also draws the eye over the river all the way to Leesburg. It's a wonderful house and setting, and perhaps that's why so many ghosts enjoy living there. For generations residents have heard footsteps in empty rooms and on the stairs. They've seen doors open and close without help from human hands. Horses have been heard galloping around the house. Loud partying has been observed in what was at the time an empty house. Name any kind of paranormal happening and it seems to have gone on there.

Annington.

Daniel Trundle, a prosperous young planter of Montgomery County, had Annington built between 1812 and 1813, probably by Charles Willson, who had built similar houses in the area. Trundle was also an active politician, serving on levy courts, county commissions, and in Maryland's House of Delegates for almost ten years. At Annington he enjoyed his growing family, but sadly, in her later years, his wife Esther, was declared incompetent. So it shouldn't be surprising to find her ghost wandering around the house and scaring people. She may not realize that she has died!

Trundle's daughter, Ann, married Dr. Stephen Newton Chiswell White in the house just before Christmas in 1823. Dr. White was a prominent local physician who also served in the Maryland State Legislature. In case you're wondering, White was named for his maternal grandfather, Stephen Newton Chiswell, a hardy immigrant who built Chiswell's Inheritance, another beautiful old Montgomery County home.

Ann and Dr. White had four children and ten happy years at Annington before Ann died in 1833. Ann and her sister, Mary Trundle Shreve, had inherited the home from their father the year before, with Ann's husband, Dr. White, given life tenancy. A future resident, Carol Caywood, felt that he may have misinterpreted it as "after-life tenancy!" Her family and other residents who lived at Annington all heard doors opening and closing and people walking in and out at all hours of the day and night. They finally concluded that the sounds were made by ghostly patients visiting Dr. White.

Several years after Ann's death, Dr. White remarried, added to his family, and built a house in nearby Poolesville. However, poor Ann's spirit was stuck at Annington, feeling abandoned and missing her four children. Now her days seem to be spent searching the house for them.

Ann's daughter, Margaret, and her husband, Robert Smoot, ended up with Annington after Dr. White moved out. They enjoyed the lovely country estate for many years, but, after the outbreak of the Civil War in the summer of 1861, their home and property were taken over by Union soldiers protecting the Potomac River and the Chesapeake & Ohio Canal; after all, a strip of Annington land had been given up in 1839 for part of the C & O Canal (see "The Chesapeake & Ohio Canal," Chapter 17). Robert Smoot was excused from service in the Union army because he was a farmer, so he and Margaret probably continued living on the property. The Confederates were right across the river at Leesburg, and the high Annington property provided a perfect Union lookout spot. On October 21, 1861, it also turned out to be a good vantage point from which to observe one of the first battles of the Civil War just across the river at Ball's Bluff.

There is an old story that Colonel Edward Dickinson Baker, the commander of the Union forces in that battle, dined at Annington on the eve of the fight. Baker was a fifty-year-old Senator from Oregon with battle experience in the Mexican War. He had been offered a commission as a general in the Union Army, but this would have required him to give up his seat in the U. S. Senate. He chose to stay in the Senate and keep his old rank of colonel. Nevertheless, he was itching to get into the fight. Baker never did anything by halves; he was a full-steam-ahead man. He intended to take the fight to the Rebs. At dinner that night at Annington, looking forward to the battle, he was quoted as saying, "Tomorrow night I will dine either in Leesburg or in Hell!"

Unfortunately, Col. Baker could not dine in Leesburg the following evening as he was killed about five o'clock that afternoon in the Battle of Ball's Bluff. After fighting all day, the Union was losing the battle and Baker's death completely demoralized the troops. They fled en masse down the one hundred-foot bluff and into the Potomac, all the while pursued by Confederates firing down on them. It was a complete rout of the Union forces (see "The Battle of Ball's Bluff," Chapter 9).

However, the ambitious Col. Baker, never one to give up, seems to want to fight that battle again. More than one hundred years after the battle, two workers at Annington noticed a man wearing an old-fashioned uniform riding a black horse across the lawn and meadows. Over the years other people have heard hoof beats as the colonel gallops down to the river, hoping to reverse the outcome of that fatal battle. He has been heard clomping up the stairs and striding down the halls of Annington, boot heels clicking. This seems to be Col. Baker's ghost, but if you want to see a more solid image of him, just head to the United States Capitol and look for his statue standing in the rotunda.

In 1901, Annington was sold out of the Trundle/White/Smoot family and then changed hands several times. At one point, Captain William S. Parkins, who had been a cavalry officer in World War I, owned it. It was appropriate for Captain Parkins to be living at historic Annington, as he was president of the Montgomery County Historical Society from 1949 to 1951. While living there, he and his family experienced all the usual ghostly sounds of the old house. A son, Robert Parkins, told of hearing "walking" noises, but he thought it was more likely to be Dr. White than Col. Baker. He remembers Dr. White's former office door often drifting open even though it had been sturdily latched. Perhaps some ghostly patients slowly leaving? Robert said he would miss the sounds if they disappeared.

Eventually Drew Pearson, the famous muckraking columnist and friend of President Lyndon Johnson, became interested in Annington. He lived just down River Road at Merry-Go-Round Farm, named for

his acerbic column, "Washington Merry-Go-Round." By this time
Annington was quite run down, but Pearson hoped to renovate it and
make the property into a self-supporting farm. After fixing up the old
slave quarters, he rented that building to the John Normans. The main
house was still vacant, but one night the Normans heard a noisy party
over there. There were lights, the tinkling music of a piano, and shadows
of people dancing. By the time the Normans managed to get over to
the old house all was dark, quiet, and gloomy. They didn't know what to
make of it. Could it be ghosts reliving Ann Trundle and Stephen White's
wedding party? Might it be Col. Baker celebrating the night before his
big battle? Who knows?

Unfortunately, Drew Pearson died before he could finish rebuilding
Annington and his widow, Luvie Pearson, decided to sell the place. Enter
the James Caywood family. What they found at Annington was a very
fine example of early nineteenth century architecture just begging to
be restored to its earlier glory. Arguments in favor of restoration were
fireplaces with original mantels in every room, two-inch thick floors made
of rare Carolina long leaf pine, hand-hewn oak beams, doors with their
original brass rim locks, and decorative plaster work that included a Federal
eagle medallion above the front hall chandelier. In addition, half of the
windows had the original glass. The Caywoods couldn't resist it. They
bought it and, with the help of their children, spent two years restoring it.
They were determined to make it as historically accurate as possible.

We could imagine the resident ghosts shouting, albeit silently,
"Hooray!" However, that's not to say that strange things didn't happen
during the renovation.

Workmen saw the soldier riding that black horse — "a funny-looking
old guy in a military uniform!" Three of the Caywood children heard hoof
beats at various times, but were never quick enough to see the Colonel.
One night, right after it had been freshly installed, a third-floor window
fell out of its frame and bounced far out onto the lawn — yet it never
broke! This window came from the "travelers' room," a tiny room with a
sloped ceiling, typical of what was traditionally offered by homeowners
to stray travelers in the early days when inns were few and far between.
Could some itinerant wanderer have liked the place so much that his
spirit stayed or was the window thrown out by an unhappy house slave
who had been quartered up there and now felt he or she had to haunt
the place? What were those strange "whooshing" noises in that area that
could never be pinned down? No one knew.

Years later, Joey Caywood, a daughter-in-law who was house-sitting
temporarily in that very same room, heard a loud crashing noise of
glass breaking. It scared her because she was alone in the house, but

she gathered up her courage and went looking for broken glass. She searched the entire house, but she never found any. Did the ghosts want people to remember that window falling out? Or was it supposed to break originally? All we know is that you can count on ghosts to do crazy things.

Despite all the spooky happenings during renovation, in 1974 the Caywoods moved in with their five children, an Irish setter, and two cats. At first the animals would refuse to go up the stairs. They would balk at the bottom with hackles raised. There was something there! The children were equally worried by the creaking stairs, slamming doors, strange walking noises, and clicking boot heels. In addition, clothing and jewelry would disappear and then reappear in an entirely different part of the house. Once they thought a skirt was lost for good until it turned up under a mattress! Some things never did come back. Carol Caywood had a childhood picture of her mother on her bedroom dresser. When she left the room each morning it would be properly placed, but when she returned it would often be facing the wall! During some periods this would happen every day. Sweet little Mother certainly didn't deserve that. Could the ghost of Ann Trundle White want only her own children to be remembered in this house? After all, she hadn't even lived long enough to see them grow up.

Though they had been told of ghostly happenings in this house before they moved in, the Caywoods didn't really know what to make of all this. It was only after Carol researched the history of the house that they began to understand that some of the former residents had never left. This became more obvious one night when a daughter awoke to find a woman all dressed in black standing at the foot of her bed staring at her. As the daughter sat up in bed, the woman turned and just walked right through an outside wall! Research revealed that there had once been a sleeping porch there. A second daughter, Beth, even heard her name being called one time by a strange female voice. Was it Ann calling to a child, or was it the incompetent Esther?

Another time Carol was sitting in the kitchen peeling apples for a pie when she noticed the knob on the closed hall door turning. The door had been completely latched, and there was no breeze. Carol watched as the knob kept turning until it was unlatched and the door slid open. There was no one there! No one was in the hall or anywhere around!

Another curious thing happened in the early 1980s. Daniel Trundle White, a direct descendant of Dr. Stephen Newton Chiswell White, visited and later asked Carol to take a photograph of Dr. S.N.C. White's gravestone. When Carol went to Beallsville Cemetery to take the photo, she realized that she was taking the picture on March 13, the exact date that Dr. White had died! Spooky!

Visitors to Annington who are attuned to paranormal conditions always cite an "aura" that persists in the house. They say they feel any number of definite "presences." When the Caywoods lived there, they finally decided to just accept the ghosts, whoever they were. Live and let live! (Or the reverse?) They decided to enjoy them. When things went wrong or disappeared, they just blamed the ghosts. Very handy!

Annington Guest House

BY
KAREN
LOTTES

Sheila didn't know what to think when her seemingly normal rocking chair started to have a mind of its own. What she thought was a quite ordinary and very comfortable rocking chair had taken to independently moving around her house. It didn't happen every day, but even just one voluntary move by a rocking chair on its own behalf might be considered unusual.

Annington Guest House, ca. 1950, was formerly the slave quarters for Annington. *Courtesy Montgomery County Historical Society.*

The trouble started soon after she moved into the Annington Guest House. On one of her first nights there, she heard a noise while in bed reading. Initially she ignored it, thinking it was nothing, but the sound got louder. When she went to investigate, of course there was nothing wrong. "Mice," she thought to herself and went back to bed. The next morning, after going downstairs, she began her usual morning routine; this included turning on the stereo. When she went into the dining room, however, she was shocked to see that a little lamp had been moved across the room to the exact spot where she would step to turn on the stereo!

Sheila had heard stories about the old plantation house, Annington (see previous story), but none about the Guest House. After discovering the history of her charming historic home, it made sense that some paranormal activity might be happening there. What had been remodeled into a lovely modern home had once been slave quarters for Annington. In Montgomery County, it is easy to forget that prior to the Civil War one-third of the County's population was enslaved and that a majority of landowners were slaveholders. Housing developments now sit where large plantations once reigned supreme. If anything remains of the historic landscape, it is the "big house," the master's dwelling. Most slave housing has disappeared as its substandard construction deteriorated and its architectural legacy was fleeting. The Guest House at Annington is an exception to this. Euphemistically called the "Quarter for Servants" in the 1857 fire insurance papers for Annington, the building housed generations of enslaved African Americans. The reason the slave quarters survived at Annington is that the structure was well constructed of brick. Originally built as two attached, two-room dwellings, over time it was combined to make the pleasant home it is today.

The owners of Annington built a plantation house that was representative of the wealthiest housing in early Montgomery County, but is not necessarily typical of the homes built by large and small landowners (although it is the type that tends to remain today). In her 1832 book, *Domestic Manners of Americans*, Frances Trollope described a farm she visited near the Great Falls in Maryland:

> One of these families consisted of a young man, his wife, two children, a female slave, and two young lads, slaves also. The farm belonged to the wife, and, I was told, consisted of about three hundred acres of indifferent land, but all cleared. The house was built of wood, and looked as if the three slaves might have overturned it, had they pushed hard against the gable end. It contained one room, of about twelve feet square, and another adjoining it, hardly larger than a closet; this second chamber was the lodging-room of the white part of the

family. Above these rooms was a loft, without windows, where I was told the "staying company" who visited them, were lodged. Near this mansion was a "shanty," a black hole, without any window, which served as kitchen and all other offices, and also as the lodging of the blacks.

We know very little about who actually lived in the Guest House or, more significantly, who died there. However, we know a little about how the slaves at Annington were treated through the oral history account of Philip Johnson. In September 1937, Mr. Johnson was interviewed by the Work Projects Administration's Federal Writers' Slave Narrative Project. The WPA sent historians around the country to interview former slaves that were still living. Philip Johnson was the only former slave interviewed who grew up in Montgomery County. He didn't live at the Annington Guest House, but we do get a sense of his life as a young slave living and working on the Annington estate.

> I was born in December, 1847...I was born down on the river bottom about four miles below Edward's Ferry, on the Eight Mile Level...I belonged to ole Doctah White [Dr. Stephen White's first wife and later his daughter owned Annington]...He owned a lot of land down on de bottom...Yes sah, Doctah White was good to his slaves...Missis took me away from de bottom when I was a little boy, 'cause the overseer he was so cruel to me. Yes sah, he was mean... We all like the Missis...She would come ridin her horse down to de bottom with a great basket of biscuits. We thought they were fine... We always had plenty to eat, such as it was. We had coarse food, but there was plenty of it...

Haunted houses often become so because of a tragic event that took place there. What could be more tragic than people living their entire lives without the freedom to come and go at will or do what they wanted? The story of their lives, and often their names, frequently go unremarked in the historic record. We have no idea how many people actually lived in the slave quarters. If we assume life for the slaves at Annington was similar to life at other farms with slave quarters of the same type, then each side of the slave quarters most likely housed one family.

One of those families may have been the Peters who were listed in the 1870 census along with Annington's owners, the Smoots. Also listed was the Grandison family. As with many places, emancipation following the Civil War did not always mean freedom for the formerly enslaved. Having no money or education, many had no choice, but to stay where they were and work for the same family that had held them in slavery.

Under such circumstances, it makes sense that the presence haunting the Annington Guest House would be mischievous, getting into the sorts of harmless trouble not allowed in life. With so many little incidents happening, the evidence mounted that the Guest House was clearly haunted. One night Sheila came home from the movies to find her rocking chair had moved so it sat in front of the door, as if someone was awaiting her return. As remarked before, the rocking chair must have been a favorite object because it moved with regularity. Perhaps the ghost finds it as comfortable as does Sheila.

The only incident that could be seen as "scary" happened to a guest. One night Sheila had a house guest staying over. He was sleeping in the living room on the sofa. During the night he awoke with the sensation that a heavy weight had been placed on him and he couldn't get up — or rather it wouldn't let him up!

When her mother was visiting over Christmas, the ghost played a little trick. As they were gathering her things to leave the next day they couldn't find the airline ticket. Everyone tore the house apart looking for the ticket, but it was nowhere to be found. The next morning, there it was, on the floor by the Christmas tree, in plain sight!

Joey Caywood knew long before Sheila that the Guest House was haunted. She had lived there years before and had, along with her husband, been responsible for its restoration. It was barely livable when she and her husband moved in, but they turned it into a cozy home. What wasn't cozy was the sound of a baby crying that haunted her off and on, day and night for many years. The crying, which was very loud and insistent, sounded as if it was coming from the upstairs, but when she went upstairs it sounded as if it was downstairs or outside. She was never able to track the source of the crying baby. Joey had heard that there was a young child who had lived at the Guest House who had been killed by a tractor and wondered if it was his ghost. Although, in a place that was once home to slaves, it was likely that more than one child had died there.

There also was the sound of a horse and wagon. In the rural western edge of Montgomery County, the Potomac Hunt was very active. Therefore, Joey was familiar with the sound a group of horses makes running the fields and roads. This sound, however, was one of horses and wagon or carriage wheels turning. Whenever it happened, she would go out to see, but the road and drive were always empty — no horses, riders, or carriages to be seen.

Once, when a girlfriend was over, her friend went upstairs — and came running back down immediately. "Who is that old black man outside the bathroom?" she wanted to know. When they went up again, of course there was no one there. Was this perhaps one of the home's former inhabitants paying a visit?

While all these things were disturbing, none of them were particularly dangerous. The only potentially dangerous thing that happened was the time her daughter fell down the basement stairs. This was a full tumble, head over heels, to the bottom. Joey went running down, scared to death that her daughter had been seriously injured. Fortunately, when she reached her, she wasn't hurt. Did the ghosts cushion her fall? Were they actually watching out for her?

These are just a few of the many inexplicable events that have happened in the Guest House. However, both the Caywoods, and later Sheila, grew used to the ghost (or possibly ghosts). They all loved the Guest House; Sheila wouldn't think of living anywhere else.

REGION IV
CENTRAL COUNTY

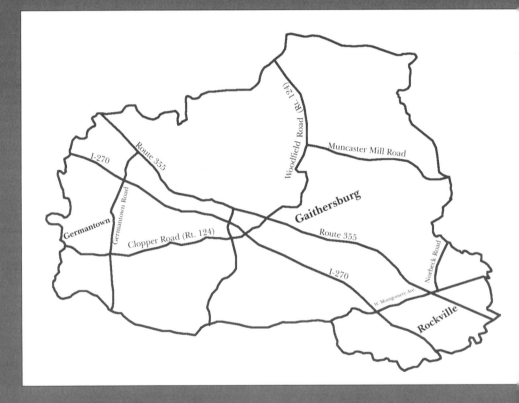

Chapter 12: Clopper

The Headless Horseman of Game Preserve Road

BY
KAREN
LOTTES

Montgomery County Sentinel, 17 March 1876

The people in the neighborhood of Clopper's Mill in this county have been very much excited for several weeks past by a mysterious occurrence which transpires nightly about 9 1/2 o'clock upon the railroad bridge over Big Seneca Creek. It is reported by those who have witnessed the strange scene that about the hour named a lantern which is upon a post planted at the bridge is suddenly darkened, the light being entirely shut off and a flame like a flash of lightening shoots straight up into the air while another of a similar character flashes directly across the bridge. Several nights ago a body of citizens numbering about fifty headed by several bold and venturesome young men armed with guns who doubtless had fought many battles with imaginary beings and were not afraid of an army of ghosts, proceeded to the bridge to solve the inexplicable mystery. They had not waited long before the hidden hand began its strange work and just as the lantern darkened the undaunted young men fired and were answered by a shot from the bridge. We do not charge that anybody ran away but no more shots were fired. It is an indubitable fact that this strange scene occurs as many men who will have witnessed it will testify. It has been observed upon moonlit nights when if any person had been in the vicinity of the lamp or upon the bridge they would have been plainly distinguishable.

We have not witnessed it as we know not whether it 'be a spirit of health or goblin damned' and do not care to trust ourself in the presence of such 'questionable shapes' but you who are not afraid of ghosts would doubtless be repaid for a visit to it. We hope that a solution of this affair will soon be discovered and a cause of terror be removed from the superstitions of that vicinity.

This was the first written report of an unearthly apparition at the railroad bridge off Game Preserve Road near Clopper. The story has its beginnings during the Civil War, before there was a railroad, let alone a railroad crossing or bridge (the Metropolitan Branch of the B & O Railroad came through Montgomery County in 1873). The story is that a soldier was decapitated during a saber charge in a skirmish, and his compatriots hastily buried him in an unmarked grave. Unfortunately, they could not find his head, and he was buried without it. Needless to say, generations of children have grown up in the area around Seneca Creek knowing there was a headless man or a headless horseman haunting the crossing and stretch of track at Game Preserve Road.

Either way, it is clear that shortly after this event, residents began to comment on the supernatural occurrences. They would hear hoof-beats of a horse galloping through the night. The jangle of spurs and the clash of swords tell the tale of a ghostly battle which continues today.

One of the most ghastly stories comes from shortly after the end of the Civil War. In October 1866 a local farmer and his family were returning home one evening along Clopper Road in their horse and buggy. Suddenly a large horse with glowing eyes appeared before them in the road. The figure that sat astride the horse leaned down and wrote something in the road. Then he rode off and disappeared. In the road was written "I cannot rest until I become a whole being." To their horror, the words were written in blood. The next day the farmer and his family disappeared, never to be seen again (*Gazette Newspaper*, October 28, 1992).

The other strange thing is the number of tragic deaths that have occurred on this stretch of railroad since the stories began. All of them involve beheadings of one kind or another. Most recently, two terrible events have continued the mystery that surrounds this stretch of track. In May 1973, a railroad brakeman on a northbound freight train innocently stuck his head out the window. The boom of a passing southbound train had broken free as the train swung around a curve. The brakeman was struck in the head by the boom, killing him instantly. The accident happened just south of the railroad bridge across Game Preserve Road, and in May 1982, a man was decapitated by a southbound train heading to Washington, D.C. as he tried to hop a car. The man, Gene Sylvester Cann, was trying to escape police after he shot and mortally wounded Jean Harvey of Gaithersburg.

Were these men just the most recent victims of the headless horseman? In their dying moments did the ghostly specter appear before them? We will never know what they saw, but generations of Gaithersburg youth, like those from 1876, continue to go to the bridge to see if they can find the Headless Horseman — and when those lights come down the track, with no train to explain their existence, we know the Horseman still rides today.

Chapter 13: Derwood

Needwood

FROM
VIVIAN
EICKE

Perhaps it is the age of Needwood that dictates it be haunted. Perhaps it is because its previous residents had lives filled with tragedy. Whatever the reason, there is no doubt it is one of the most actively haunted buildings in the county.

Historic Needwood Mansion can trace its history to the original 1,000-acre land patent named "Needwood." This patent was granted to John Cooke in 1758. Over time pieces of the property were sold off and the land was resurveyed. In 1813, William Robertson married Harriett Cooke, the granddaughter of John Cooke. Robertson purchased 759 acres in 1832, land that would later be known as "Sunnyside."

Needwood Mansion, formerly known as Sunnyside.

Robertson deeded the 759 acres, along with numerous buildings, to his son, William George Robertson, in 1842, the same year William George had built and moved into a one-and-a-half-story log structure he named Sunnyside with his bride, Mary Victorine Key Scott, of Baltimore. The Robertsons prospered, and in 1856, William George built the center brick section of the mansion. By 1861, the Robertsons had twelve children, three of whom died as infants, and twenty-one slaves.

On June 26, 1861, tragedy again struck the Robertsons. William George had been inspecting his fields when a thunderstorm blew in. He galloped back to his mansion trying to outrun the storm. Just as he arrived at the front walk, both he and his horse were struck by lightning, killing them both. He left behind his widow and nine living children, with child number thirteen on the way. Mary Victorine continued to live at Sunnyside and struggled to run the plantation, raise ten children, and deal with the hardships of the Civil War. Her eldest son left in 1864 to ride with Confederate Colonel John S. Mosby. It was said that Mosby's men would occasionally stop by the house during raids in Montgomery County.

By 1880, Mary Victorine had sold the property to George Washington Columbus Beall for $8,500. Beall immediately burned down the slave quarters. To family and friends Beall was known as "Lum" and was said to be a cantankerous individual. Once, he got into an argument with a neighbor and chased him down the drive with a shotgun. Luckily, knowing her husband's temperament, Lum's wife had judiciously removed the shells from the gun. Although his family remembered him fondly after his death, it wouldn't be out of character for him to not want strangers in his house. After all, he wasn't friendly with them when he was alive, why would he want them disturbing him when he is dead?

Following Lum's death, his sons Frank and Edward ran the farm. They obtained a patent for an all-purpose medicine and built a factory on the property to produce it. The medicine was made from plants grown on the farm. The Bealls owned the property until 1947, when it changed hands several times before being purchased by the Maryland-National Capital Park and Planning Commission to be used as Park offices. Reports of odd happenings began almost as soon as Park and Planning moved into the house.

Over the years, Park employees working in the mansion have experienced a variety of hauntings. There is even a police report on one. In 1961, before the building was occupied, a Park Policeman had stopped by the house one night after having driven by and found the lights turned on. He entered the building and turned off all the lights and locked up before heading home. After he left the mansion, he looked back and saw the lights come on again. When he looked at one of the upper floor windows, he could see a woman looking through the window. He immediately re-entered the building and searched it thoroughly, but could not find the woman or a reason for the lights to be on again.

Regular reports of lights flickering or turning off and on by themselves are just some of the manifestations of the haunted building. Doors that open and close themselves, crashes and footsteps can also be heard throughout the house. A secretary who was working late one night said someone grabbed her and spun her around, but no one was there.

A park manager, after working alone late at night in the mansion, turned off the lights and left through the rear door, locking it behind him. While driving down the driveway, he noticed a light on in the front office. He turned around and went back. Instead of going into the building, he looked through the window of the rear office that opened on the front office. What he saw was startling. He described a woman in Victorian dress walking through the open doorway between the offices and turning out the light. Could this be Mary Victorine Robertson taking care of her house?

Another employee was working in his office on the second floor and had brought his dog to work that day. His dog had been peacefully snoozing next to his desk, but began staring intently at the door that stood between what were once two bedrooms. As the employee looked over in the direction of the door, he saw it open by itself and close again. This door had been locked!

In the early 1900s, one of the servants discovered she was pregnant and her lover abandoned her when he found out her condition. In those days, it was a terrible scandal for a child to be born out of wedlock. As with many women at that time who found themselves in a similar situation, ostracized by society and cut off from friends and family, she took her own life. Her family found her in the kitchen in a pool of blood; she had shot herself in the head. It is believed she was the cook or a member of the kitchen staff. On occasions, the staff has smelled breakfast being cooked or chocolate cake being baked, but when the stove in the kitchen is checked it is cold. Could this be the young servant girl going about her duties?

An employee was working late one evening down in what used to be the mansion cellar. Being the only one there, she had just the cellar lights on. She was finishing up some data entry before an evening meeting to be held at the mansion when the lights went out. Thinking she had blown a breaker, she went to get her car keys so she could get a flashlight out of her car. Rummaging around in the dark she finally found her purse. Although she remembered that she had put the keys in the purse and had zipped the purse shut, she couldn't find them. She continued to feel around on the tables, but still couldn't find her keys. Making her way into the next room, she ran into one of the showcases that houses artifacts and, while feeling her way along the showcase, found her keys. She left the mansion, locking the door behind her figuring that she would get something to eat and come back. If the lights were still out, she'd have to cancel the meeting. When she returned every light in the mansion was on, with those coming to the meeting waiting outside. As it turned out, some maintenance men had accidently cut power to the mansion, but who took the keys out of the closed purse and moved them to another room? Did they get a supernatural laugh out of seeing her stumble around in the dark?

Sometimes a house, which is home to one spirit, is better attuned to new spirits as they leave the earth. It is clear that Needwood, which very early in its life became the home of one specter, could easily have become a magnet for others that also wanted to stay.

Walter "Wat" Bowie

BY KAREN LOTTES

A Metro Station is a strange place in which to find a ghost. The Metro Station at Shady Grove was only built in 1984, but it sits over Rickett's Run, the site of a little-known Civil War skirmish, the Battle of Rickett's Run, that occurred October 7, 1864.

During the Civil War, Montgomery County was divided politically, as was most of the country. As Maryland was a southern state, Montgomery County had many slave owners and southern sympathizers living here, particularly in the western part of the county and the Medley District, the voting district which encompassed Poolesville and the Potomac River crossings. Many county citizens crossed the river to fight for the Confederacy.

The eastern part of the county tended to have more Union sentiment, particularly the area around Sandy Spring and Olney, which had a large Quaker population. By 1820, the Quakers of Montgomery County had freed all their slaves and had even made it possible for the free African American community in their area to start their own church, Sharp Street United Methodist, which was founded in 1822. In the presidential election of1860, Abraham Lincoln only received fifty votes in Montgomery County, most of them from Sandy Spring.

The story starts quite a distance from Montgomery County in Port Tobacco, Charles County, Maryland. There, eight members of Mosby's Raiders, led by Walter "Wat" Bowie, had crossed from Virginia into Maryland with the intention of kidnapping Governor Augustus Bradford of Maryland and holding him for ransom. It seems that several Confederate agents had been captured by Union troops while helping Bowie escape during a previous raid, and he felt obliged to them and wanted to somehow negotiate their freedom. Kidnapping the governor seemed a good way of achieving that goal, though in hindsight the plan was clearly ill-conceived. After commandeering some horses from local Federal troops, the group was on its way to Annapolis.

Unfortunately, they found that their little group was no match for the amount of protection surrounding the governor, so an alternative plan was formed. Bowie, having come from the area, was very familiar with the back roads of Prince George's and Montgomery Counties. He decided to lead the group west, where they could easily cross the Potomac near Poolesville, an area where he knew he could get assistance from its sympathetic residents. On the way they stopped to pick up Bowie's brother Brune at their home, Egglington, near Collington in Prince George's County.

Walter "Wat" Bowie was from Montgomery County, but joined up with Mosby's Raiders, a Confederate unit.
Courtesy of the Sandy Spring Museum.

As the group passed through Sandy Spring, they saw a well-stocked store and decided to take advantage of the situation. The town of Sandy Spring was well-known for its affluent and peaceful Quaker residents, and Bowie probably thought there would be no resistance. Shortly before midnight on October 6, he banged on the door of the store, waking the owner Alpin Gilpin, his family, and the store clerks. While Gilpin tried to stall what he thought were common thieves, a few of his men went out the back and around the store in an effort to surprise the soldiers. Unfortunately, they were the ones surprised, as they were surrounded by the Confederates. Bowie and his men then proceeded to basically take what they wanted from the store before they resumed their journey west toward Poolesville.

As reported in the *Annals of Sandy Spring*, what happened next was "an occurrence of a different character. It is one so anomalous, so outside the long, even tenor of Sandy Spring, that the recital might be omitted as being an exception; but the truth of history makes an irresistible claim for the statement of facts just as they occur." Gilpin, unlike the typical image of a Quaker, did not take the crime sitting down. He immediately went to the local sheriff. Under his leadership, a posse of fifteen residents was formed to go after the criminals. An indication of the community's outrage at the crime was that the posse was made up entirely of Quakers—all of them armed! The posse eventually ran the soldiers down at Rickett's Run on the Rickett farm at what is now the intersection of Crabb's Branch Road and Redland Road.

A fierce battle quickly ensued. The Raiders, who were taken by surprise, made a brief stand and then fled the scene, taking only what they could easily grab. When the smoke cleared, the only wounded were a horse and Wat Bowie, who was taken to a nearby farmhouse and left in the care of his brother Brune while the rest continued on to Poolesville. Bowie died shortly after. Over the years, his ghost has been seen walking the site of his final — and worst planned — military engagement. Following the construction of the Shady Grove Metro, Wat Bowie's ghost has remained. He probably feels it wouldn't be right to be chased off by some newfangled construction when Rickett's Run remains.

To read more on the Civil War in Montgomery County, we suggest *Civil War Guide to Montgomery County, Maryland* by Charles Jacobs.

Chapter 14: Gaithersburg

Herman Rabbitt

FROM
SUSAN
SODERBERG

Not too long ago a woman named Carol bought a brand new house in a new development in Gaithersburg. This was her dream house for which she had worked very hard and where she planned to operate her business out of the basement, so she was not very happy when strange things began to happen in the house.

A few weeks after she had moved into the house and had everything unpacked and arranged to her satisfaction, she and her fiancé went out to dinner. When they came back about an hour later, they went upstairs and found that all of the furniture in the bedroom had been piled in the middle of the room. At first she thought is was a prank being played on her by her son, who was in the Army. Despite the fact that he was in another state she thought maybe he had been able to sneak home for a joke. When she reached him by phone the next day he said he had been home all night.

Nothing happened for a few more weeks, but then one day, while she was in the basement with a client, she heard a lot of noise coming from the floor above. "Like someone was having a party in my kitchen," she said. When she went upstairs she found that her potted plants, which had been arranged on a plant stand, were all lined up diagonally across the kitchen floor.

Another time she came out of the shower to find that a magazine stand which usually stood next to her bed was in front of the bathroom door blocking her way. She would regularly find other pieces of furniture moved around the house. She accused her fiancée and her visiting son of the displacement of the furniture, but they adamantly denied it and had alibis. What at first seemed like an annoying but harmless prank began to appear to her in a new light.

Shortly before she and her fiancée were to go away on a cruise, they found the dining room furniture piled into the middle of the room — just like it had been in the bedroom — and then, while they were on the cruise ship, the situation took on new dimensions. A fellow voyager on the cruise who was a clairvoyant looked into Carol's eyes and said, "There is a man in your house walking around and looking for something. He is moving furniture and looking under and behind things in his search. He is old and stoop-shouldered and hasn't shaved in a few days. He is wearing a plaid flannel shirt and an old overcoat." Carol figured this had something to do with all the strange happenings in her house. If everything that was happening could be blamed on a ghost, who was he? When Carol got back home, she contacted a friend who had some knowledge of local history and told him her story. He knew right away who it was, as there was only one person who fit her description.

According to everyone who knew him, and many who didn't, Herman Rabbitt was quite a character. He used to buy the unwanted stock of local farmers — old milk cows, male calves, unpromising heifers, etc. — and fattened them up, then shipped them to Chicago via the railroad. Many locals were familiar with the sight of Herman driving his cattle down local roads to transfer them from one field to another or to take them to market, avoiding the cost of trucking. Herman was really big on saving money. He also had a distrust of banks, having taken a loss during the depression, and had gotten into the habit of burying his money, in the form of silver coins, in old milk cans around his farm. He had plenty of money, but you would never know it to look at him. He wore old farm clothes wherever he went and was particularly fond of his old black overcoat, which he held together with pins because it had lost all its buttons. He just didn't care what other people thought. A friend related how he was once almost thrown out of a Chicago hotel as a vagrant until someone recognized him, and then he was given VIP treatment.

He wasn't stingy with his money, though. Many a local farmer was saved from bankruptcy by a timely loan from Herman, who only asked that you pay him back when you could. He was loyal to his friends, but had a great distrust of strangers, banks, and the government. He didn't like to pay taxes either.

Herman lived on one of his farms in a ramshackle old Victorian house with no indoor plumbing or central heating. Being a bachelor all his life he liked it just fine, but his housekeeper, Bessie Mills, complained. Bessie finally gave him the ultimatum that she wouldn't work for him anymore unless he moved or remodeled the house, so he had a new brick rambler built across the road from the old house. The basement of the new house was cement except one corner where he buried his money. One neighbor said he could remember seeing Herman moving his milk cans in a wheelbarrow by lantern light late at night for three nights in a row. He didn't like the new house much and friends would find him sitting in the old house or the barn, always ready for a visit with his familiar greeting, "Hey Boy!"

No one knew exactly how much money Herman had or where it was all hidden. Some say that even Herman had a hard time remembering all of his hiding places. Whenever anyone ventured to ask him where his money was, Herman would say, "Whoever gives me my last drink of water will know that."

Herman never got to tell anyone, at least not as far as anyone knows. He died of a heart condition on October 10, 1972. More than $540,000 in cash and $250,000 in silver coins was found in an old oil drum and milk cans at his home place. No one knows if that is the extent of his holdings. After the sale of his three farms, his estate was worth well over two million dollars. His housekeeper, Mrs. Mills, sued for a portion of his estate, saying the money was promised to her in an earlier will, but she lost out to Herman's old cattle trading buddy Charles Rau, who inherited most of the estate. About ten years after Herman's death, the home farm became a housing development and the old house was torn down. The brick rambler, however, became part of the development and is still there. Carol's house was built exactly where the old house had stood... She now knew who was haunting the house.

However, she still hadn't seen the ghost or actually seen anything move — until that one sunny morning when she was vacuuming her living room and all of the music boxes in her collection suddenly turned on all at once. Then the rocking chair moved from one side of the room to the other right before her eyes, leaving ruts in the carpet as if it was much heavier than it really was. She ran out of the house to a neighbor's and began making phone calls right away. There was no way that she was going back into that house until Herman Rabbitt had vacated it. She finally found a Baptist minister who was willing to perform an exorcism.

The minister came and sprinkled holy water on all of the walls of the house, laying his hands on the walls, saying prayers, and demanding that the ghost leave the house. Since that time Carol says that there have been no more incidents of moving furniture, much to her delight and peace of mind.

However, there have been some reports of a hunched-over figure in a black overcoat roaming the nearby fields on a moonless night — going back and forth over a certain area as if he was looking for something... his treasure, perhaps? After all, there's no telling, really, if all of Herman Rabbitt's buried treasure has ever been found.

Chapter 15: Germantown

Richter-King House and George Atzerodt

BY KAREN LOTTES

There is a relatively new house in Germantown where mysterious things have happened. The owner, a policeman, feels the house shake every time he puts on his dress blues. Heavy footsteps are frequently heard going up the stairs. What could have happened to haunt this house?

Richter-King House, 1974, is no longer standing.
Source: Montgomery County Historic Preservation Commission.

The answer lies not in the house, but in where the house stands. It is on the foundation of an older house — a house with a history of fear attached to it. It was the Richter-King House in Germantown, which played host to George Atzerodt, one of the Lincoln conspirators.

The story actually begins on Friday, April 14, 1865, in Washington, D.C. George Atzerodt met with John Wilkes Booth, Lewis Paine, and Davy Herold to plan President Abraham Lincoln's assassination. Booth's plan was not just to murder Lincoln, but Secretary of State William Seward and Vice-President Andrew Johnson as well. Each member of the group was assigned a role to play in the plot. The task of killing Johnson fell to Atzerodt. This was news to Atzerodt as he had agreed to participate, thinking it was merely a plot to kidnap the President. He didn't realize how far Booth's fanaticism went.

George Atzerodt.
Source: Library of Congress.

Atzerodt prepared for his task, but at the last minute his courage failed. He went to the Kirkwood Hotel, where Johnson was staying, but detoured through the bar, hoping to "drink up" some courage. In the end, it failed him and he fled the hotel. Going back through the city, he went first to Herndon House, where the conspirators had met, and then toward Ford's Theatre. Passing 7th Street and Pennsylvania Avenue, he saw that Booth had acted — the President had been shot!

While Atzerodt was wandering the city, wondering what he was going to do, he met up with a stranger, Sam Thomas. They struck up a conversation and eventually Thomas invited Atzerodt to share his room at the Pennsylvania House. During this time Atzerodt came to realize he had to get out of town.

The next day Atzerodt began his journey to upper Montgomery County and to the home of his cousin, Ernest Hartman Richter. The house had been built in the 1850s on a farm that had been jointly purchased by Henry Atzerodt and his brother-in-law John Frederick Richter. John Richter eventually bought out Henry Atzerodt, and later his son Ernest had taken over the farm. George Atzerodt had frequently visited and was well-known in the neighborhood. He thought his cousin's farm might afford him safe haven while he figured out what he should do next and so he began the thirty-mile trip on foot.

As Atzerodt walked through Georgetown, he stopped at the store of John Caldwell, where he used his revolver as collateral on a $10 loan. He also stopped to have breakfast at the home of Lucinda Metz, to whom he was known as Andrew Atwood. He then decided to take the stage north.

As the stage approached Tennalytown (aka Tenallytown or Tenleytown), he saw military pickets. To avoid the pickets he left the stage and eventually met up with a farmer heading to Gaithersburg. He was able to get through the pickets in the farmer's wagon. From Gaithersburg, he continued his walk north, arriving near Barnesville around 11 p.m. He stopped for the night at the Old Clopper Mill.

Sunday morning, Easter Sunday, Atzerodt continued on his way, stopping to eat the midday meal at the home of Hezekiah Metz. Also there were Somerset and James Leaman, who brought up the subject of Lincoln's assassination. Atzerodt spoke reluctantly, but knowledgeably about the assassination—enough so that it aroused the suspicions of Metz and the Leamans. Atzerodt was unaware of this as he continued to his cousin's. There, he stopped for a few days, hung out, and helped with the farm chores.

On the morning of Wednesday, April 19, at five o'clock, Atzerodt was roughly awakened by a blue-clad soldier sticking a pistol in his face. His revelations about the assassination three days earlier at Hezekiah Metz's had come back to haunt him. Through a network of spies, the information had worked its way to the 1st Cavalry stationed at Monocacy Junction. Once under arrest, the military moved him to the Old Capitol Prison in Washington, D.C., where he was eventually hanged.

Those heavy footsteps are, no doubt, the soldiers coming to arrest Atzerodt — and it's Atzerodt's spirit that shakes as he fears the soldiers in blue coming to get him.

To read more on the Lincoln Assassination, we suggest "They Shot Papa Dead!" in *The Road to Ford's Theatre, Abraham Lincoln's Murder, and the Rage for Vengeance* by Anthony Pitch and *The Trial: The Assassination of President Lincoln and the Trial of the Conspirators* by Edward Spears.

Chapter 16: Rockville

Beall-Dawson House

In the center of Rockville sits the Beall-Dawson House. Originally built in 1815, the house is now the home of the Montgomery County Historical Society and is a museum. The period rooms illustrate life in Rockville during the early 1800s, and changing exhibits explore different aspects of Montgomery County's history. The house is a two-and-one-half-story Federal-style home with a kitchen/slave wing attached. It is also haunted.

BY KAREN LOTTES

OPPOSITE PAGE: Beall-Dawson House, 1936, showing the front porch, which was added onto the house after 1890. *Source: HABS, Library of Congress.* **ABOVE:** The Beall-Dawson House as it appears today.

The fact that museums often seem haunted isn't unusual. After all, they are unoccupied much of the time and lighting is often very dim or almost non-existent. When you are alone in the Beall-Dawson House at night and you walk up the stairs and see a body before you, it can take a second for your heart to stop hammering and for you to remember it is just a mannequin, part of the current exhibit. You feel a little embarrassed. A rational person knows that old houses creak and historic house museums, which are often empty and lonely places, can seem even creakier than most old houses. However, the Beall-Dawson House *is* haunted. On more than one occasion, psychics have walked through the house with gaussometers, devices that detect the electromagnetic force (EMF) that a ghost creates. These fields have been found in the most obvious places, such as over the electrical box, and the most unlikely places, such as the barely electrified archway area.

It is in the archway area that an actual ghost sighting took place. In the 1980s, one of the volunteers was working in the room called the Old Kitchen (so called because it was the original kitchen for the house). Looking through the doorway into the area called the Archway she saw a man working on the brick floor. He was a black man wearing rough clothes kneeling on the floor laying the bricks. He shouldn't have been there and, when she called to him, he disappeared.

Who was he? The Bealls, for whom the house was built, were slave owners and the house was most likely built with slave labor. The archway is an area between the main part of the house and the kitchen. It was originally open on one side, creating a modified fire break between the two spaces. The floor was brick, laid in a herringbone pattern in sand. In the mid-1940s, the house was bought by the Davis family who restored it. They re-enclosed the open arch, which had been badly enclosed at some earlier indeterminate date, and decided that they would rather not have sand in the middle of their house. The bricks were taken up and re-laid in the same pattern, but with cement. Could our unknown ghost be the enslaved bricklayer who put the floor down almost two hundred years ago? He had to have been a skilled craftsman who took pride in his work. Could it be frustrating his spirit to have those bricks in cement? Or could it be Nathan Briggs, the bricklayer who reset the bricks in the 1940s. He committed suicide shortly after finishing the job. Could his troubled soul be haunting the site of his last job?

Two other events also illustrate the haunting of this old house. One weekend day, when there were no visitors to the museum, the volunteer docent heard a noise that sounded like someone walking through the house. She went through to make sure all the doors were locked and that no one had come in unexpectedly. The doors were locked and the place was empty. Later in the afternoon she again heard someone walking through the house. She again went to investigate. Again, there was no one, but a dish that had been on a side chest was now in the center of the dining room table, its normal resting place.

On another occasion, one of the staff was working in the museum at night. All was quiet as she tried to get her work done. Suddenly, she heard a voice calling "Priscilla." Who would have been calling Priscilla? Amelia Somervell Dawson and her husband John Dawson lived in the house with Margaret Beall from 1870 until Margaret's death in 1901. Margaret was a feisty and determined businesswoman who was born in the house in 1817 and lived there her entire life. The three Dawson daughters, Margaret, Mary, and Priscilla, inherited the Beall-Dawson House from her. Could it have been Miss Margaret calling Priscilla Dawson?

Who can say if an old house is haunted or just creaky? Those who have worked in the Beall-Dawson House have often felt a presence when there was no one there. They were certain there was someone behind them looking over their shoulders, but there never was. The worn, old floors would never let a more corporeal body sneak around. It's just a feeling...

Rose Hill

BY
KAREN
LOTTES

One wouldn't expect to see little green men in Rockville. After all, this isn't Ireland, but such was the case at "Rose Hill" in Rockville.

Over the course of its life, since being built around the 1750s, Rose Hill has had many owners. The Beall family owned it for a significant portion of the nineteenth century, and it was the Rev. John Mines, husband of Eliza Beall Mines, who named it Rose Hill. He was a poet and it probably appealed to his artistic sense to have a proper name for the house. The name is first mentioned in the December 1832 obituaries of two of its residents, Susan Shippen Mines, age twenty-seven, and T. J. Mines, age one year, four months. Such young deaths are tragic and can often create an atmosphere conducive to ghosts.

Our little green men aren't recorded until the twentieth century, after the home was purchased by the Dawson Family. The Dawsons purchased Rose Hill in 1914, but may have rented it prior to that time. When Catherine Dawson was five and had been living at Rose Hill for some years, she awoke one morning to the sight of little men dressed in green playing with her toys. She always knew them to be friendly and was never afraid of them. However, they were not her playmates, as she only watched them. She never actually interacted with them.

Catherine's younger sister, Carter, saw them years later. She was much younger than Catherine, having been born in 1925. She recalls seeing them peeking around a corner, which proved a delightful sight for the young girl.

We don't have any reports of activity from the Bullards, who lived there starting in 1935. Perhaps the extensive renovations they did disrupted the little green men and they decided to leave. Perhaps the Bullards didn't have the same Irish roots as the Dawsons. Whatever the reason, they seem to have left Rose Hill.

Rose Hill.

Glenview Mansion

BY DOROTHY PUGH

The people of Rockville, Maryland, and the surrounding area are very lucky to have the Rockville Civic Center Park in their midst with its wide-range of available activities. They can view theatrical productions in the F. Scott Fitzgerald Theatre, visit the Croydon Creek Nature Center, use the playgrounds and tennis courts, climb a wall, have a picnic, or just wander the grounds. They can also tour Glenview, an elegant mansion of more than thirty rooms that hosts regular art shows and is available for weddings, receptions, conferences, and other gatherings.

Glenview Mansion is the centerpiece of the Rockville Civic Center Park.

All these wonderful activities take place during daytime and early evening hours; but other stranger things sometimes happen in Glenview after hours. There can be weird sounds in different parts of the house. Sometimes the lights come back on after being turned off for the night. Things will disappear from a desk and then reappear somewhere else. The employees have taken to saying that those things have been "borrowed" by the resident "borrower," whoever he or she may be. Then there was the time a worker saw an indentation appear on the seat of one of the black leather benches that are scattered throughout the mansion. He actually saw the leather go down! Ghosts get tired, too. One employee has regular eerie experiences when her calculator will begin running all by itself. Could it be a ghostly accountant unhappy with the park's numbers?

One time a caretaker was locking the doors on the second floor, which needed to be done for the security system to work. He shot the bolts on two doors and was turning to the remaining ones when he heard a noise behind him. The first two doors were standing wide open! The caretaker decided to do his own bolting and left! He said there was a weird feeling in the air, and he didn't want to stay up there any longer.

Another time a different custodian went into a room in the basement — and the door slammed shut behind him. It was locked! If that wasn't bad enough, then the light went out. The lights were controlled right in that room, but the custodian couldn't get his light back on. There were people in other parts of that large building, but they couldn't hear him shouting. Finally, the lights came back on and the door opened. This happened at least three times.

There seems to be a force afoot in this mansion that sometimes pushes people around and even immobilizes them. The same custodian who had the incident in the basement was upstairs waiting for a downstairs event to finish when he suddenly was pushed down on a couch and felt a weight settling on top of him. He couldn't see anything, but he couldn't get up either. He eventually fell asleep and, at some point, must have slipped onto the floor because that is where other mansion employees discovered him the next morning.

On another night, an alarm went off. Police responded with a K-9 dog. While investigating the upstairs, the dog went on "point." He became very alert, then tore off and raced downstairs, through a hall, down more stairs to the basement and ran right into a wall! Then he backed up and began barking at the wall until he suddenly stopped, put his tail between his legs, whimpered, and crept back up the stairs. He adamantly refused to go back down into that basement. One officer reported, "Yep, couldn't carry that dog back down there."

Another time there was to be an outdoor event on the grounds. An assistant director of the mansion's theater camped out there for security reasons in a small zipped-up tent. Suddenly he was awakened by a tremendous wind blowing right through the tent, causing the sides to flap wildly. At the same time the director found he couldn't move, "When I woke up, the only thing I could move was my head. I felt like I was really weighted down." He could hear horses galloping around the tent. They went round and round, and when the wind finally stopped, they ran off. He said, "The weirdest thing was the wind. There was no way such a wind could have come in." When he could move again, he went out but found nothing, not even hoof prints. Research revealed that a previous owner had pastured a race horse in that field. Ghost horses?

The original plantation house here was built by Richard Johns Bowie in 1838 and was called Glen View. Richard Bowie was the grandson of Colonel Allan Bowie, Jr., who was a close friend of George Washington. In fact, Richard's father was named Washington Bowie because George was a sponsor at his baptism. Our Richard Bowie was also a first cousin of the renowned Allan Bowie Davis of Greenwood (see "Greenwood," Chapter 2). Richard was no slouch himself, being a state senator, a U.S. congressman, and eventually Chief Judge of the Maryland Court of Appeals, forever after known as Judge Bowie.

In 1863, the confederate Major General J. E. B. Stuart came through Rockville on his way to join General Lee at Gettysburg. Besides capturing a valuable wagon train of supplies on Rockville Pike, General Stuart also took some hostages, including Judge Bowie, who was in church at the time. (These little activities delayed the arrival of Stuart's cavalry at Gettysburg, thus depriving Lee of his "eyes and ears" when he needed them. Some think if Stuart had been there earlier, the South might have won that battle.) Most of these hostages were released at Brookeville that evening, but Judge Bowie and some others were forced to travel with Stuart another day (without food) until they were finally let go at Cooksville, Maryland, near present-day Route 40.

Although the Judge worked his plantation with more than twenty slaves, he was a solid Union man. At one time he was involved in an organization that was encouraging African Americans to go to Liberia, but the effort died because of lack of interest.

Judge Bowie and his wife had no children, but they shared Glen View with two nieces. With the prestige of the Judge and with beautiful young ladies in residence, the old mansion saw plenty of parties and social activities until the Judge died in 1881 at age seventy-three. He is buried right across the street in the Rockville Cemetery.

By the time the name Glen View had evolved into Glenview, it was owned by Irene Moore Smith, who married Dr. James Alexander Lyon. Together they added elaborate sunken gardens to the grounds and greatly enlarged the mansion. There was even a very handy dumbwaiter installed.

The Lyons had one child, Betsy, whom they must have doted on, as they built a large story-and-a-half playhouse for her. It had a kitchen, fireplace, spiral staircase to a loft, a sleeping porch, and a full basement. It was known as The Doll's House, but in reality it could house a family, as it later did — a couple and their daughter. In the main house, Betsy had a playroom and her own bathroom. Her bathroom was special, having two toilets, one for the "big people" and one for the "little people." These parents thought of everything!

We are not sure who the ghosts are that inhabit this house, but we might mention that the mother, Irene Lyon, died in the house. Also, the pampered daughter, who grew up, married three times, and was widowed twice, was not happy with her life. Down in her Washington apartment one day she turned on the gas, but neglected to light it. Perhaps she's come back, seeking to recapture the happiness she had here in her very special childhood.

We can't forget Judge Bowie who is just across the street. Perhaps he doesn't like the huge expansion of his old plantation house. We must also remember that he sent many criminals away for their natural lives. Could they be bringing their unnatural lives back to the Judge's old home?

Many people have been intrigued by the ghostly stories of old Glenview, but most don't research it as thoroughly as Joy Nurmi did. Joy was a reporter for the *Gazette* newspapers and, in two separate years, she spent a night in the mansion. The first year she and another reporter experienced three strange happenings. At 2:30 a.m. there was a loud thud somewhere in the house. They investigated, but could find nothing out of place. When they returned to their original room, they found the gas fire in the fireplace had gone out — and yet the gas was still on! Remember Betsy? Finally, the next morning, twenty minutes before the employees were to arrive for the day, the locked back door mysteriously opened! They had tied a chair to the door so they would know if it moved. They heard the crash of the chair, but could find no one around.

Intrigued, the next year Joy went back with more people, including two psychics, who definitely felt a "bad presence" in the house. One also felt a cold spot just outside a "deep room" in the basement that can only be accessed by a small, child-sized door. At some time during the evening they all went out to look at The Doll's House. The "cold spot" psychic said she saw a ghost there; a man wearing only shorts stooping down near it. As they were returning to the main building, a large piece of slate came crashing down from the roof right in their pathway! Was the daughter annoyed that they were investigating her special place? I don't think the reporters have stayed there again.

Old Mr. Clint

FROM ANNA PICKARD

It was in 1903 when Mr. Henry Clinton Allnutt bought the thirteen-year-old, elegant Beall House in the newly fashionable West End Park in Rockville. This ten-room Queen Anne Victorian with a wrap-around porch was full of modern conveniences, such as wiring for electric lights, water from a windmill at Henderson Circle, and even a speaking tube from the second floor to the kitchen. The Allnutts were a prominent family in Rockville with Henry Clinton serving as Registrar of Wills in Montgomery County for many years.

The Sante House is also known as the Beall House.

Fast-forward sixty years to 1963; the house was now owned by Julian (Pete) and Margaret (Peg) Sante, who lived there with their five daughters. When they first learned that someone else might be living in the house, it was not, in fact, a dark and stormy night. It was a bright, sunny morning, and Peg was in the kitchen making breakfast when she called upstairs to the third floor to wake up two of the girls, Beth and Peggy. She told the sleepy one, Peggy, to stamp her feet to let her know that she was really getting up. The sound of stamping feet came clearly from above and, when Peg called up "Good Morning," a muffled reply was heard. However, to Peg's surprise, a few minutes later both girls walked in the back door! They had just returned from a slumber party that Peg had forgotten about.

Who was upstairs? When Peg told the story to an elderly neighbor, she heard about "Old Mr. Clint" (aka Henry Clinton Allnutt), who had lived in the house for forty years and had died on the third floor in the quaint, fish-tail-shingled, square tower — right where the girls were supposed to be sleeping. Rather than being shocked, Peg loved the thought that her house might have a resident ghost. Every year she thoroughly enjoyed celebrating Halloween by serving visiting trick-or-treaters "Bat's Blood with Floating Eyeballs" and telling the children about Old Mr. Clint who lived in the tower.

Sadly, Peg has passed on, but Pete insists that she has joined Old Mr. Clint. Pete often talks to them both and feels they answer by opening and closing doors, making strange noises, switching lights on and off, and creating messes that he then has to clean up. Peg had filled her lovely, old home with precious antiques, each with its special place. Pete has found that when he moves one, he often finds it right back in the place Peg had picked out for it. Pete will fuss and fume, but what can you do with ghosts? At least he's never lonely in "Old Mr. Clint's" house.

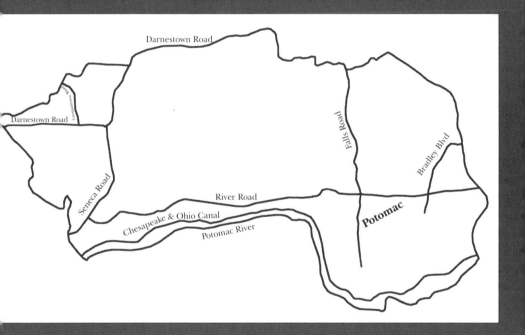

Chapter 17: Great Falls

The Chesapeake & Ohio Canal

BY DOROTHY PUGH

This picturesque, artificial waterway follows closely along the Potomac, a mighty river that flows from the Piedmont plateau through waterfalls and rapids, out to the Chesapeake Bay, and on to the Atlantic Ocean. The river should be a great conduit for trade and transportation, but those falls and rapids forbade ships from getting much farther inland than a few miles beyond Georgetown. What to do? George Washington, who loved the Potomac and owned many inland acres, came up with a solution — build short canals around those rapids and falls. He organized the Potowmack Company, which built several small canals and even a supporting town called Matildaville in Virginia. However, this venture was never completely successful and, in 1828, its charter rights and privileges were turned over to the newly organized Chesapeake & Ohio Canal Company, which created the C & O Canal that we know today.

The C & O Canal came into being on the Fourth of July, 1828, when President John Quincy Adams stuck his shovel into the ground near Little Falls. He struck roots twice before finally hefting a shovelful of dirt and that may have been a portent of the bad luck that has dogged the Canal ever since. This canal was planned to go from Georgetown all the way to the Ohio River at Pittsburgh, some 360 miles. The actual final canal, containing seventy-four lift locks, ended at Cumberland, Maryland, 184-1/2 miles away. Coal, wheat, and other produce were hauled by barge on the canal from the northern regions to Georgetown. Each boat was pulled by two mules plodding along the accompanying towpath.

Today many people feel the canal is haunted. Spectral and misty figures have been seen up and down its length. A few have been identified, but we're going to have to guess at some of the others.

Boat being towed along the Chesapeake & Ohio Canal, ca. 1900.
Source: Library of Congress.

It took twenty-two years to build that big ditch to Cumberland, and there were plenty of accidents and deaths along the way. The canal workers were a rowdy bunch, loving their whiskey and their fights. The canal company also made the mistake of hiring men from two warring Irish clans, the Corkonians of County Cork and the Longfords of County Longford. There was open warfare between them with so much killing and maiming that at one point Federal troops had to be called in to keep some sort of peace. Some people think that the ghosts they see along the Canal could very well be these clansmen still fighting it out.

In addition to this, there was a severe cholera epidemic in 1832. One worker reported forty men dying in two hours! Some lucky men survived this terrible disease, but most that developed it died. They are buried all along the canal. Some lie in the small, graveyard on a hillside near the Great Falls Tavern where ghosts are regularly sighted.

Other spectral images can be seen along the canal near Leesburg, Virginia, where the Civil War Battle of Ball's Bluff was fought (see "The Battle of Ball's Bluff," Chapter 9). Ghostly figures have been known to rise up from their graves in the small, walled cemetery there and fiercely skirmish all over again. Old time canal boat captains said it wasn't wise to tarry in that area at night. "If you stop, you'll hear them." A new captain once tied up there and found that his mules were so nervous and restless that they wouldn't eat. Then his boat's shore line came untied. As soon as he caught his boat and fixed that, he heard sounds of the hatches opening. Upon checking, he found them still tightly closed. His young mule driver finally informed the captain that he was tied up in that ghostly area commonly called "Haunted House Bend," and maybe they should move. They moved upstream a mile, and all was serene.

Plenty of other Union ghosts may be seen along the canal as bodies from that battle came to rest as far as fifty miles downstream. Reflecting the other side of the conflict, a shade of a Confederate soldier has been seen near the Monocacy Aqueduct searching for a lost Union payroll. Almost a year after Ball's Bluff, in September 1862, the Rebs crossed the Potomac near the mouth of the Monocacy River, surprising the Union forces. In the general rout, the payroll was lost and never found. The Confederates added to the Union misery by wreaking great destruction on the canal.

We should also remember the many slaves that followed the canal as their route to freedom. It proved to be a handy road for them as its name assured them of a clear path north.

There was also the lock tender who enjoyed showing off his collection of rare coins to the boatmen who came through. Not a good idea! He was found one morning inside his burned lock house with his head smashed in. The coins were missing. His murder remained unsolved until months later when one of his coins showed up in a saloon along the canal thirty miles away. The man proffering it was arrested, quickly found guilty of murder, and hanged. Canal justice! Did the lock tender's angry spirit entice the murderer to go to that saloon where the coin could be recognized? One would like to think so.

Another saloon was the Salty Dog at Shantytown, the roughest, toughest part of Cumberland, where an old-timer said it was a rare day when there wasn't a fight and someone wasn't pulled out of the canal with his head bashed in. Surely some have come back for revenge.

The following is a condensed version of an interesting ghostly experience near the canal as recounted by a boatman named Pic in *Life on the Chesapeake and Ohio Canal*, published in 1859 and edited by Ella E. Clark and Thomas F. Hahn:

> Dare is ghosts. I've seed em wid me own two eyes. One night when
> I wuz comin' home past dat old cellar hole where dey say de squaw was

murdered, der was a loud BOO! My hair stud straight on end! Dare wuz a ghost standin' on de heart' stone in front of dat ole fireplace!" When asked what he did next, Pic replied, "I jus' angulated my legs an' run! I cud feel dat ghost's breat' on de bak a' me nek and heah his great hoofs clomp clomp ova' de stones. I t'ought ev'ry minute he wud put his paw on me and dat I wud be fugaciously destroyed!"

Luckily Pic managed to outrun the big, hairy spook and reached home, scared and "ex-hoss-tocated." Bottom line: Be very careful along that canal at night!

One of the saddest ghosts is the sweet little Jenkins girl who drowned in the canal and who can now be seen skipping along the towpath all the way to the Paw Paw Tunnel, a place that has been described as "long, dark, spooky, and dank, with water dripping from the ceiling."

However, not all of the spooky images are people or big hairy beasts. There have also been sightings of ghostly barges floating silently along in the dark — probably steered by specters of former boatmen looking for the joys and excitement of the old days on the canal.

Other hauntings might come from the many deaths and injuries that occurred when storms, hurricanes, and floods knocked out bridges, locks, and even walls of the canal. Mother Nature seemed determined to shut it down. The Baltimore and Ohio Railroad, begun the same day as the canal, was happy to help. It gradually took over much of the carrying trade from the Cumberland area, especially when the canal had to shut down due to floods. Finally, in 1889, a tremendous flood caused such massive destruction that the canal company was forced into bankruptcy. Despite all efforts to keep it open, there was another disabling flood in 1924. The working canal was finished.

Years later there was a movement to change the canal into a two-lane parkway, supposedly so people could more easily enjoy the beauty of the area. The commuters would have loved it. Luckily that proposal failed, primarily due to the efforts of Supreme Court Justice William O. Douglas, a dedicated conservationist, who for many years led an annual trek the entire length of the canal. Thanks mainly to him, we have The Chesapeake and Ohio Canal National Historical Park today, the only national park sporting a canal.

Now it is our sad duty to report that one kind of manifestation is missing from this tale. No filmy, misty, spectral mules have been seen plodding along the towpath — yet.

If you want to read more about the C & O Canal, we suggest *The C & O Canal Companion* by Mike High and *The Chesapeake and Ohio Canal* by Mary Rubin.

The Tommyknocker

BY
KAREN
LOTTES

Gold, ghosts, and the United States Capital! Who would have thought that there were gold mines so close to the Nation's Capital, let alone "TOMMYKNOCKERS!" You may not know that there is gold in Montgomery County, but there is! Gold was first discovered here in 1829, and by 1849 Samuel Ellicott had turned part of his farm, near Olney, into a working gold mine.

Maryland Mine showing the processing mill, ca. 1905.
Courtesy Montgomery County Historical Society.

During the Civil War, William Clear discovered gold in the Great Falls area when his unit, the 71st Pennsylvania Infantry, was encamped by the Potomac in the fall of 1861. He, and others who knew of his discovery, returned following the war. They bought land, formed the Maryland Mining Company, sank a fifty foot shaft, and began mining. They were able to send gold to the U. S. Mint starting in 1867. Soon gold fever took hold, and many gold mines opened in the county, most of them in the Great Falls area.

The Maryland Mine, originally opened by William Clear and his partners, was the longest lived of the gold mines and is located just off MacArthur Boulevard near where it meets Falls Road (near the Great Falls entrance to the C & O Canal National Park). The early, fifty-foot shaft was used into the 1870s, but later other productive shafts and tunnels were also sunk into the earth. Underground, the miners used candles, and later they wore helmets with oil-wick lamps for safety and to provide light. New shafts were opened in 1890 and in 1903.

Tragedy struck on the night of June 15, 1906. Two miners, George Elliott and Charles Eglin, were preparing a box of dynamite to blast an addition to the existing underground tunnel.

The Maryland Mine following an explosion, 1906.
Courtesy Montgomery County Historical Society.

At about 10:45 p.m., they were gathered in the hoist house with their lit oil-wick lamps on their helmets and their box of dynamite. The story was that they had been taking sips from a Georgetown bottle (a bottle of whiskey bought at a Georgetown saloon) before going underground. The box of primed dynamite was put down on a bench, and one of the miners put his helmet beside it. They were caught up in talking and drinking when suddenly one of them noticed that the dynamite wick had caught fire! The men ran. There was a tremendous explosion which could be heard for miles around. George Elliott barely escaped, but the hoistman, Charles Eglin, was killed instantly as the building collapsed.

Almost immediately after the tragedy strange things began to happen around the mine. A story began to spread of a Tommyknocker or miner's ghost that had taken up residence at the Maryland Mine. A Tommyknocker is a miner's ghost who remains at a mine after the miner's accidental death. Folklore characterizes a Tommyknocker as always having glowing red eyes and a long tail. Miners tend to be superstitious already, so these miners no doubt had to build up their courage to go back into the mine.

Was Charles Eglin's ghost there? No one knows for sure, but old-timers verified that horses would balk when getting near the mine after the explosion. One horse named Liz would snort and rear up on her hind legs. There was no way her driver could get her past that gate!

The night watchmen felt it too. One said he could hear footsteps coming up the gravel path right to the office door, but when he opened the door no one was there. Another would hear knocks on the door, but again no one was on the other side. No one knew what was causing this peculiar behavior until one night. It was sometime after the accident when the custodian of the Maryland Mine, Edgar Ingalls, got a phone call around 2 a.m. from the night watchman who was in a panic.

"Get over here quick," yelled the night watchman. Ingalls jumped on his pony, Teddy, and galloped the mile to the mine as fast as he could. The watchman was shaking with fright, Ingalls recalled years later. "A ghostly-looking man with eyes of fire and a tail ten feet long crawled out of the shaft and disappeared into the forest... I started to shoot, but remembered the tommyknocker could throw the shot back into my face. Mr. Ingalls, I ain't doing this job anymore!" Ingalls recalled the watchman exclaiming.

After that it was almost impossible to get night watchmen. The mine closed in 1908, although it did re-open briefly in 1913, again in 1915, and for the last time in 1935. Mining operations had ceased altogether by 1939. Ostensibly it was because needed investment capital could not be obtained, but the difficulty in getting good miners because of the Tommyknocker certainly contributed to the mine's problems.

Remember, if you are near MacArthur Boulevard and Falls Road late at night and you see some red lights in the woods, you had better get out of there… The Tommyknocker is on the loose!

To read more on gold mining in Montgomery County, we suggest *Montgomery County Gold Fever* by Walter Goetz.

Great Falls Tavern

BY
DOROTHY
PUGH

One of the most spectacular sights in Montgomery County is the Great Falls of the Potomac. It's thrilling to watch the white-flecked, foaming water come roaring through a narrow, rocky gorge. It's exciting! It's eye-popping! It's also tragic, though, as many have lost their lives in the water here; six drownings each year is the average. One of the saddest and earliest we know of happened back on July 10, 1894, during a lovely sunny outing to the falls when Evans Fugitt fell in the river and drowned. He was about to become engaged to Anna Farquhar, daughter of the well-known Quaker, Roger Brooke Farquhar of Rockspring Farm. Evans' body was never found, and Anna never married. Might she be one of the wraith-like souls floating over the falls, still looking for Evans? Or have they found each other and are haunting their own "special place" right here at the falls?

Great Falls Tavern, ca. 1950, also known as Crommelin House.
Courtesy of Montgomery County Historical Society.

Although we hear more about the deaths in the river, the bordering Chesapeake and Ohio Canal has had its own share of accidents and drownings (see "The Chesapeake & Ohio Canal," this chapter), so it shouldn't be surprising to find ghosts in this vicinity. Besides those of drowning victims, the spirits arise from deaths suffered down through the years — some of the sturdy men who helped build the canal, Civil War soldiers, gold miners, hard-drinking boatmen, and probably even some long-gone park rangers — and they all seem to hang out in the Great Falls Tavern, now a National Park Service Administrative and Interpretive Center.

The park rangers have had some really spooky experiences in this old building. One ranger came in early one morning and saw someone sitting at one of the desks. She thought he was merely another employee until she noticed that he wore old-fashioned clothing, complete with one of those ancient high collars and wasn't anyone she knew. In fact, he was a little hazy, and as she was puzzling it out, he just disappeared from sight! Another ranger, also coming to work early, looked through a window and saw the back of someone who was talking on the telephone. That shouldn't have been unusual, but that room was padlocked, and when the ranger unlocked the door, the room was empty! There was a superintendant who usually came in early before the public was allowed in the building, and he would often hear the shuffling feet of people on the stairs of this one-time hotel, but no one ever came down. In recent days a face has appeared in an upstairs window — again in an empty, locked room. More than once! The room is the library, where high, crowded stacks of books create a gloomy, twilight atmosphere, a perfect spot for a ghost reliving days gone by. Another time a ranger once went to open a door, but the knob turned in his hand, and the door was violently pulled open. There was no one on the other side. What a feisty bunch of spirits!

Among the first ghosts to consider would be the canal workers, who died of accidents, fights, and cholera. Some were Irishmen who were always spoiling for a quarrel, especially if their fellow workers were from another clan. Cholera got a lot of them, too, as is evidenced by the small graveyard on a hillside near the tavern. Some of the graves were marked with stones, most of which were primitive, and are mainly gone now. Of the fourteen that remain, some may be foot stones. Only three have any marks that can still be read. One has a small "d" and a small "p" above a capital "L." Another just has "T. O'R." Maybe one of those Irishmen named Timothy "O'Rourke?" The third one is marked "Sacred to the memory of Matthew Rayner, Stonecutter of Pudsey, Yorkshire, England, who died July 13, 1855, aged 25." This one is beautifully done;

so appropriate for a man whose occupation was stone-cutting, but it's so inappropriate for him to have died so young. There is no information about cause of death.

The Great Falls Tavern started out in 1828 as Lockhouse #12 beside Lock #20 on the canal, but it grew into something much more, becoming an inn for travelers on the canal and for visitors from Washington by 1830. It was originally called Crommelin House after Dutch bankers who helped finance the canal. There was even a ballroom on the first floor and a "honeymoon suite" up on the third floor. In 1831 a canal engineer's report stated, "At this lock we found an excellent hotel kept by Mr. [W. W.] Fenlon. The house…is a necessary and great accommodation to those who visit this interesting work." The tavern served overnight guests, lunch guests, and "grog" guests.

Most lock-keepers up and down the canal also provided the boatmen with "grog." In addition, many barge owners bought their own supplies from Mr. A. H. Bradt's store in Georgetown, where they could be sure to obtain the celebrated "Horsey Whiskey" from Burkettsville, Maryland. The unfettered, ever present drinking of the canal men created such wild behavior that in the summer of 1848 the canal company ruled that no intoxicating liquor could be sold along the canal. (Might some of our spirits be looking for some of those other, long-gone spirits?)

When the Library of Congress lost most of its books in a fire at the Capitol in 1851, the powers-that-be in Washington realized that the District of Columbia had to have a more reliable source of water. Where else but from the Great Falls? (There were people at that time who maintained that it was the greatest source of power in the country!) Work was begun on a huge nine-foot-diameter pipe just north of our tavern. A substantial gatehouse of brick and stone was built, in addition to a large frame barracks for the workers. After years of digging following the curves of the river, the Washington Aqueduct made it all the way to the District, where it still provides water for the Washington area (see "Cabin John Bridge," Chapter 20). They built a road on top of it with the descriptive name of Conduit Road, now changed to MacArthur Boulevard, which still follows the aqueduct curves. This is truly a "street paved with gold" because it was built of gold-bearing quartz from the Great Falls area. With the various mishaps related to the building of such a gigantic project, who knows what workers' spirits might still be floating in and around that twisty, turning pipe and road? Be sure to keep your car doors locked at night!

In 1861, the Civil War broke out with Johnny Reb and Billy Yank charging back and forth across the Potomac. Sometimes Confederate spies even stayed at the tavern right there in Union country. A gun battle back and forth across the river at Great Falls took place at the beginning of the war, in early July 1861. Two young D.C. Volunteers, George Riggs and Martin Ohl, were killed in the day-long engagement. Ohl's last words were for his wife, asking her not to grieve for him; that he died for liberty and his country. It wouldn't be surprising to find the patriotic Ohl's ghost still at the tavern, looking for those spies. He's surely joined by other phantom soldiers whose bodies came to rest near the tavern after floating down the river from the Union carnage up at the Battle of Ball's Bluff near Leesburg (see "The Battle of Ball's Bluff," Chapter 9).

We're not done yet! Right after the Civil War, when the presence of gold in the Great Falls area was publicized, a frenzy of uncontrolled gold fever broke out. Men were wildly panning and digging all over the place. Mines proliferated. One of the most productive, the Maryland Mine, was right up the hill behind the tavern, and although it has its own unusual ghost (see previous story), some haunts from other mines might still be hanging around looking for their big strike.

Remember that large barracks built for the aqueduct workers? Well, about this time it was converted into a saloon and café. Alcohol was prohibited on canal property, but this building was a few feet east of it. Since this saloon could sell spirits, it became quite lucrative for the owner and also quite notorious. The gold miners loved it. They ate, drank, and fought there. A few may even have died there. Perhaps some of those are still around trying to settle old grudges.

Actually, the real heyday of the canal itself and the tavern was a bit later, after about 1870 when as many as one hundred boats a day would go through the locks, and there were special packet boats for passengers who would stay at the hotel. During this period, Howard A. Garrett, sensing great commercial opportunities, not only operated the tavern, but was involved in building a feed store, a mule stable, and several other buildings. The little hamlet soon boasted a grocery store, blacksmith shop, ice house, waterworks, and even a post office. By the 1910s, a trolley line, the Washington and Great Falls Railway, ran out from D.C. with a turnaround near the Tavern. It was a sort of "Toonerville Trolley" in that the passengers sometimes had to get out and walk up the hills. On quiet days the conductor and motorman amused themselves by shooting rabbits and collecting chestnuts and blackberries along the way. The trolley is long gone now, but Bradley Boulevard follows some of the roadbed.

During this period, the tavern was quite the social center with groups of every kind meeting for sport, debate, religious instruction, or just a good time. Back then, as now, it was a popular picnic spot. Great Falls Village was booming! However, time brings change, and today all of those commercial enterprises are gone. They have totally disappeared! The only buildings remaining are the stone gatehouse and another one built for the aqueduct and the old tavern. A ghost town without the town! No wonder there are so many haunts around. It's a natural for them!

The tavern fell into disuse and became so dilapidated that demolition was considered, but the popularity of the Falls induced the Park Service, which now owned the building, to renovate it and use it as an interpretive center. For a few years around 1950, the Montgomery County Historical Society used it for meetings and kept one of the rooms furnished as a typical lockhouse room of the 1830s. Today the Park Service has a small museum in what was once the ballroom.

When you think of the complicated history of this spot and all the people who have died in different ways near this tavern in its almost 200-year existence, it's a wonder that there aren't more ghosts around disconcerting the park rangers. Maybe there are and we just don't know it — after all, the Park Service makes everyone leave at dark....

To read more about the Tavern and Lock-houses on the canal, we suggest *The Chesapeake and Ohio Canal Lock-houses and Lock-Keepers* by Thomas Hahn.

Chapter 18: Potomac

Bradley
Boulevard Farmhouse

BY
DOROTHY
PUGH

There used to be a creaky, old farmhouse out along Bradley Boulevard that was believed to be inhabited by the spirits of long-ago occupants. In the 1950s, one resident respected those ghostly beings enough to have even declared in his work biography that he lived in a haunted house. Unfortunately, he gave no details of why he believed that.

The house is gone now, replaced by a big, beautiful, new dwelling, but stories of that old farmhouse remain. Outside doors were heard to open and close, leading the owners to suspect someone had entered the house. Of course, no one had. Several times visitors who were alone in the house had felt enough of a strange presence that they left as fast as they could. "Spooky" has been the word used to describe the experience. The dogs of one new owner refused to enter the house. They eventually overcame their fear, but never seemed quite comfortable when inside. Another owner awoke one night feeling that someone was watching him. There seemed to be a shadowy figure standing in the doorway. It was no one he knew. His subsequent investigation revealed that no one was there at all.

In early 1969, Frank and Rosie Bell (Embrey) Counselman were occupying the old house. Frank died on April 11, 1969. Poor Rosie evidently couldn't live with that, so she joined Frank by taking her own life just eighteen days later. How sad it all was. Seven years after that a new owner died in the master bedroom. All of these people rest in local cemeteries, but their deaths in the old house certainly provide fertile ground for those ghostly manifestations. We must also remember that this house was said to be haunted as early as 1950, so who knows how many ghosts were wandering around in that creaky, old house. We haven't had any reports yet that these spirits have moved on into the new house, but we're watching!

Harker Prep

BY DOROTHY PUGH

For twenty-nine years there was a top-notch preparatory school tucked neatly away in a modern housing development near Tuckerman Lane and Postoak Road. Many near-by residents didn't even know the nineteen-acre campus was there, but evidently some ghosts did. They kept haunting the place, probably looking for a diploma in "Spooks and Apparitions."

They especially liked the main building, the large, old, brick house built on a hill by Henry Clagett back in 1810-1812. This was originally the centerpiece of a good-sized plantation, complete with numerous outbuildings and a tenant house, all now gone. In the 1940s and 1950s the farm covered almost three hundred acres and was owned by Colonel and Mrs. Richard LaGarde. They called their farm Highlandstone, a name preserved in a development now covering part of the farm. This was a quality farm as exemplified by the stable which had very unusual stalls built of rich, beautiful mahogany. Unfortunately, the county tore the stable down to put in Harker Drive. At least the sturdy, main building still stands, although it now sports many additions.

LaGarde Hall at Harker Prep, now known as Kiplinger House.

That old plantation house, renamed LaGarde Hall, was the heart of the school begun by retired Air Force Colonel John E. Kieffer. He started the school in 1963 with six students and ten instructors. He said, "I kept the instructors who weren't teaching busy clearing the land." By sticking to an intense curriculum and small classes, he guaranteed that all students would be accepted to top colleges and universities. The student body ranged from 50 to 125 with the average enrollment in the last years around 65. Not counting the ghosts, of course.

According to Ace Williams, a caretaker of the school and a descendant of slaves, ghosts have been wandering through the old house since the Civil War. Ace himself is gone now, but he once lived on the property, saying he went with the school, and his stories are still told. He thought one of the ghosts might be a former employee, either of the farm or the school, or even a long-gone Clagett. Who knows? It's likely that Ace himself is still around, having joined up with the other haunts rather than leave his old home. Civil War soldiers are another possibility as old bullets have been found on the grounds. In late June 1863, a Confederate cavalry crossed the river near Potomac and headed up Falls Road past the Claggett farm to Rockville. When they encountered some Union troops on the road, there was a running battle until the Union forces retreated to Washington. Some of those Confederates may still be roaming around looking for stray Federals.

A Harker administrator once heard noises in the dining room. She thought it might be branches brushing a window. The noise was loud enough that she went to check, but there was nothing near the window and nothing inside that might have made the noise.

Many occupants of the old farmhouse have heard someone walking along the upstairs central hall when there was no one on the second floor. One recalcitrant student, cooling his heels in Colonel Kieffer's office one day, heard the footsteps upstairs at the same time the Colonel did. No one was supposed to be up there. The Headmaster told the student, "Go find out who that is." It was no one and, luckily, the Colonel accepted the student's report. Another day this same student actually saw a strange-looking man in one of the upstairs windows. He was dressed in period clothing. Quite out of place! It gave the student a very odd feeling. In more recent times when this same former student walked past the old LaGarde Hall and looked up at that window, he got that same odd, creepy feeling.

Once when Colonel Kieffer was alone in the house and reading late at night in a room on the first floor, he again heard those same footsteps upstairs. His two dogs were lying on the floor beside him, and they began to whimper. The Colonel decided it would be wise to leave, and the dogs beat him out the door!

Colonel Kieffer's son, Chris, who took over as headmaster in 1983, has said, "This is a noise-causing ghost walking around. It's footsteps on a wood floor. It's upstairs, and it's not squirrels!" Kieffer has also seen a fleeting movement in a doorway up there, a shadow where there shouldn't have been one. In a typical observation of a non-believer, he said, "I'm not one to believe in these things, but it's spooky." There also were reports of students sensing a feeling of someone else being with them upstairs, and some have said they saw a ghostly apparition walking through the hall.

An ancient well that was once on the property provided its own supernatural legend. Supposedly, strange noises were heard around it, screams and splashing water. The story is that an angry husband had thrown his wife's lover in there. We're sorry to tell you that this intriguing story could not be confirmed.

Sad to say, Harker Prep is no more. It closed some years ago, but we hope the ghosts are happy to see that their haunted home is still being used. LaGarde Hall, now named Kiplinger House, is the administration building for yet another school, St. Andrew's Episcopal. This school serves preschool through grade 12, and has about 450 students. It also has a beautiful, large, new, brick building, an athletic center and fields, tennis courts and many other amenities. It is classy-looking, beautifully landscaped, a top-grade school, but one might be excused for missing sweet old Harker Prep. We hope the spooks are still there, whoever they might be!

The Garrett House

BY
DOROTHY
PUGH

There is an old house in Potomac, sitting well back from Falls Road among verdant greenery that is called the Garrett House. This house began as a one-and-one-half story log cabin in 1840 as a tenant house for a larger home on Glen Road. You can still see the logs, mortar, and beams in the dining room and upstairs in the master bedroom. Over the years this little log cabin has grown mightily with various additions and improvements until now it is a lovely, large, Victorian-style home. However, people seem to have had trouble holding on to it, with four separate owners losing the house to foreclosure. At one time it stood vacant for two years, deteriorating without proper maintenance until some brave souls bought it and spent much time and money repairing and modernizing it. They made Garrett House into the beautiful home that it is today.

A few years ago the mother of the then owner was resting on her bed. A door to the old log cabin section of the house was open. As she was drifting off to sleep, she felt something get on the bed and cuddle up next to her. It snuggled right up to her. She knew she was alone in the house, but thought it might be the family dog or cat. She moved her hand to pet it, but the space was empty. She looked down and could see nothing. She got up and checked and discovered that all the pets were outdoors! She didn't know what to think.

It happened again! And again! When she told her daughter about it, she found out that when renovations had been done several years before, strange things had gone on. Items would disappear and then reappear in a completely different place. There were other typical ghostly happenings, which the present owners have also experienced: noises, doors opening and closing, creaking floors, strange scratching noises, and the burglar alarm going off for no reason.

The grandmother's experience, though, was something different. No one could figure out what was cuddling up to her. Those owners talked to some of the local people and found out that many years before a young girl who may have lived in that house was accidentally shot and killed by a young boy who also lived there. Alice Ricketts, an eleven-year-old orphan, lived with Mr. and Mrs. Frank Karns and their eight-year-old son. One Sunday the Karns were out and the boy's grandmother was staying with the children, who were playing in the kitchen. It is thought that they were examining an old musket that was kept there when, suddenly, it went off. The boy rushed to the grandmother, shouting, "I've killed Alice!" Indeed he had, as poor Alice was dead, shot in the head. Mr. Karns had been careful to keep that musket unloaded, but had recently loaned it to a friend who had evidently returned it with a charge still in it. Mr. Karns hadn't thought to check, so this was truly a tragic accident. It seems that when there is a grandmother in the house, Alice comes back and cuddles up to her, looking for solace.

Trespasser's W

BY
DOROTHY
PUGH

Just northwest of Potomac Village, along River Road, is a pleasant old house where the resident ghosts seem to love exasperating the owners. They click light switches on and off, open barn doors that have been wired shut, drag ghostly chains up the stairs, have all-night poker games in an empty closet, make party noises in the kitchen, and have caused a seven-day clock to run for six weeks without winding! This house also once contained a secret, sealed-up room on the third floor that was discovered only because the owners noticed that there was a little cathedral-style window on the outside that didn't appear on the inside.

Trespasser's W, also known as the Capt. John McDonald House.

The original two-story log house that was located here was built in the early 1800s by Thomas Levi Offutt and was simply known as "the plantation house on River Road." Thomas Levi and his wife, Sarah, farmed the plantation. Their only child, Thomas Marshall Offutt, later had a general store at "The Crossroads" ("Offutt's Crossroads" then, "Potomac" now). The Exxon service station holds that spot today. Thomas Marshall also had a hot temper and, when Oratio Clagett put up a rival store across Falls Road, Thomas Marshall pulled out his gun and put a bullet through Clagett's hat. Thomas was arrested and jailed, but the wily fellow managed to escape. He was free for two years before being nabbed at his home by a District of Columbia bounty hunter who earned $300 for the capture. Thomas Marshall Offutt eventually died in jail.

The father, Thomas Levi Offutt, died the same year Thomas Marshall was originally jailed, 1855. We know when Thomas Levi died because his tombstone turned up in a plowed field years later, but no one knows just where his body lies. Poor Thomas Levi, separated from his tombstone, may not know where he should be and may be wandering through the plantation house, dragging chains and hoping someone will hear and answer his call for help. With a lost family graveyard, there may be other sad souls reaching out, too.

Thomas Levi Offutt, the father, did write a will, and he left most of his property to his wife, Sarah, and only $1 to his jailed only child, Thomas Marshal Offutt. Thomas Levi also left a house to Thomas Marshall's wife, Lois, with the stipulation that if she was widowed and remarried, the house would go to her children. When Thomas Marshall died some years later, Lois did remarry. However, she didn't want to give up the house, and lawsuits between her and the children continued for years.

One of those litigious children, Winfield Offutt, took over Thomas Marshall Offutt's old store at "The Crossroads," using his own tricks to stay in business. There is a story that a man rode up with a jug strapped to his saddle to be filled with liquid refreshment at fifty cents a jug, but as he rode away the jug suddenly sprang a leak! Winfield's rifle had mysteriously gone off. Not only did the rider have to fork over another fifty cents for a refill, he also had to buy a completely new jug! Guess Winfield was a better shot than his dad. These lively Offutts surely must be some of the ghosts kicking up their heels at the old plantation house.

In 1870, the new owner of the plantation on River Road was Captain John McDonald, a decorated and severely wounded Civil War veteran. Actually, it was his horse that had originally been wounded. The Captain suffered his severe injuries when the horse fell on him, but he recovered enough to become very active socially, culturally, and politically. He served in the State Legislature, was State Comptroller in 1891, and was elected the first Republican Congressman from the Sixth District of Maryland in 1896. While in that position, he formally requested a post office for The Crossroads. He was asked to name it, and, unprepared for the question, he blurted out "Potomac." It has been Potomac ever since.

Sadly, the plantation house burned down three years after the Captain and his wife, Mary, moved in. They replaced it with a fine new home for themselves and their six children, which must have greatly pleased any resident ghosts. Captain McDonald's cultural and political life seems to have precipitated a lot of entertaining in the fine new home. His record of purchases at the Offutt store included bottles of rum, whiskey by the gallon, flour, spices, almonds, figs, candy, and goblets. (Sometimes these purchases were followed soon after by ones of castor oil and asafetida, a folk medicine.) It's easy to assume that the ghostly partying in the kitchen and the poker games in the closet date to this era. (Closet? Were they trying to hide? Who was playing and what kind of poker was it?)

Captain McDonald's wife, Mary, died in 1883. Some years later the Captain took a pretty young bride, Rosa Maria Holland, otherwise known as "Mame." The Captain died in 1917; three years later Mame also died. Many years after that an old neighbor insisted he had seen her buried in the yard right where a beautiful lilac bush later flourished. Research reveals that Mame has a tombstone in the Rockville Cemetery right beside the Captain's. Could Mame be another spirit who may not know exactly where she is? Or maybe she just prefers being back at her lovely old home on River Road.

After that the house went through several owners until Newbold Noyes, editor of the old *Washington Star* newspaper, and his wife, Betty (Beppie), bought it in 1949. They named the lovely old home "Trespassers W" after Piglet's house in the woods featured in A. A. Milne's *Winnie the Pooh* stories. It's fun to speculate that the Noyes wanted to think that the strange things happening in their house stemmed from natural causes rather than unnatural ones, but the Noyes' were the ones who noticed that window that didn't show on the inside. They investigated and found a secret room that had been neatly plastered up and thus inexplicably sealed. It is in this area that a future resident kept hearing pacing from the window to a stairway and back again. Could someone have been closed up in there?

Subsequent owners were Herbert (Jack) and Carey Miller who told of having a merry old time with the resident ghosts. When they were about to enter a room, the lights would magically come on. When they left, the lights went off. They could even hear the switches being flipped. Others have actually seen the switches change. A painter working in the house once became so flummoxed by this that he dropped a whole gallon of paint and bolted out of the house, never to return. Jack Miller would close the barn door at night and find it open in the morning, so he wired it shut — only to find the door not only open the next morning, but with a stake pounded in the ground to keep it open. Theirs was the seven-day clock that ran for six weeks without being wound.

This mysterious clock, plus regular loud bumping noises in the empty laundry room (haunts washing their own sheets?), finally caused a maid to "give up the ghost" and quit. At one time, a lawyer friend who was house-sitting experienced the lights, bumping noises, and other strange sounds and vowed that he would never stay in that house alone at night again.

The ultimate spectral activity was observed by one of the Millers' sons. One night, when he was sleeping up on the third floor in the previously sealed room, he was awakened by a filmy, female wraith dressed in white Victorian clothing. She stood over him, spoke not a word, and then just faded away. The Millers felt she was Captain McDonald's second wife, Mame, because of the story of her being buried in the yard under a lilac bush. Two of Mame's nieces said that the room in which she appeared had been her bedroom. She may have died there. Carey Miller tried not to believe in ghosts, but had to admit that she was happy to have Mame in her home and observed, "I liked Mame. She kept me company when Jack was traveling."

Sadly, the time came when Carey and Jack had to leave their treasured home, although Carey didn't want to leave dear, old Mame, the friendly ghost who had made her feel so secure. Mame's lilac bush grew near the Miller's swimming pool, and the day they moved, the pool house blew up! There was some work going on there, but....

Small gravestone found on the grounds at Trespasser's W.

William and Diana Conway had admired the house for years, and when it came up for sale, they were thrilled at the chance to buy it. They already knew about the spooky tales that went with the house, so they added a condition to the sales contract. Bill, a friend, and their two dogs wanted to spend a night in the house to see if any strange things happened. Those congenial Conways wanted to be sure that the ghosts would welcome them. One of the dogs "tracked" something up the stairs, but nothing else happened, so they purchased the house.

While the house was on the market, the real estate agent had noticed those erratic lights and had an electrician check the wiring. He found nothing wrong. After the Conways bought the house, they hired an architect who knew nothing about the resident spirits. When he noticed problems with the lights, he had the wiring replaced. However, they still turned on and off without benefit of a switch being touched. When a contractor working there noticed a particular light doing this, he simply removed the bulb and left. When he returned, the bulb was back in place and once again burning. This contractor also had the good luck to see the woman in white upstairs. Could she have something to do with these lights? They are still surprising people with their unpredictable behavior.

The architect also felt strange in the formerly sealed room upstairs. The hair on his arms stood up, and he felt someone was watching. He had never experienced that before, but although initially it was frightening, he did feel the presence was friendly, sort of a guardian angel. Good old Mame?

Bill Conway had his own unique experience in the house. Late one night when everyone else was asleep, he was doing paper work in a back room. Suddenly he heard harmonica music. The radio was off. It was quiet outdoors. The music seemed to be coming from the center of the room. Strangely enough Bill could walk right around it. It was definitely in the center. It went on for some minutes, and then it stopped. Bill couldn't figure it out. Remember Captain McDonald's great parties? Perhaps a musician is still hanging around waiting for more good times.

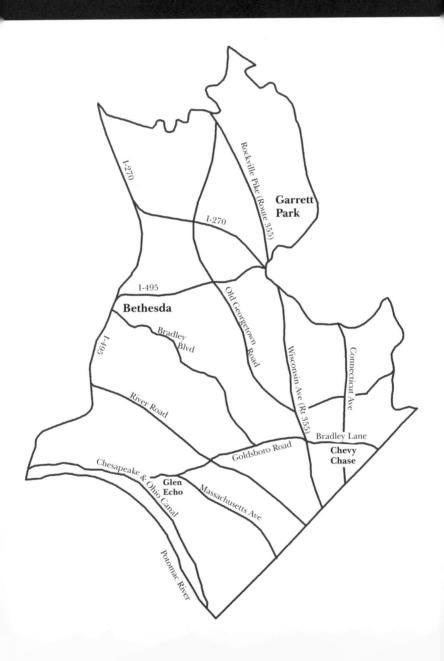

Chapter 19: Bethesda

General Braddock's Ghostly Army

FROM CLARENCE HICKEY

It was the spring of 1755. British General Edward Braddock and his troops marched through Montgomery County on an ill-fated mission that left him and many of his officers and men lying dead in Pennsylvania. If you have ever been on River Road, in the low lying areas near Cabin John Creek during the dark midnight hour, you may have seen or heard his ghostly army materialize there.

It all began in April 1755 when General Braddock was hastily summoned from his post in Gibraltar in response to a threat by the French, who were busily constructing forts along the Great Lakes and into the Ohio Valley. The French were expanding their fur trade and solidifying their presence in Canada and southward. The British considered the territory as far north as the Great Lakes as their own by right of royal grants. Braddock was placed in command of two British regiments in the Potomac valley and ordered to march north and engage the French, driving them back northward. For Braddock's troops, this was a strange, vigorous, and rough land far away from the gently rolling hills of England in which to engage in a battle. In the colonial capital of Williamsburg, it became evident that it would take a major military effort to force the French to pull back.

General Braddock and his men arrived in Alexandria, Virginia, in April to recruit additional troops and requisition supplies from the governors of Virginia, Maryland, and Pennsylvania. Braddock made the decision to send half of his forces through Virginia and the other half through the untraveled lands of Maryland to a point of assembly at Fort Cumberland in Western Maryland. In weather that was unseasonably warm and sultry, small boats ferried soldiers, horses, and supplies across the Potomac River to the opposite shore at Georgetown.

Arriving at the mouth of Rock Creek on Saturday, April 12, five miles south of Little Falls, Braddock's army began its sixteen-mile march from Georgetown. They followed the "Great Road," which roughly corresponds to Wisconsin Avenue, turning off to take River Road part of the way, and then working their way into what is present-day Rockville. The colonial Maryland countryside was sparsely settled (there were fewer than 18,000 people living in Montgomery County), yet the route from Georgetown to Frederick was heavily traveled. At that time Montgomery County was still part of Frederick County (Montgomery County was created in 1776). Georgetown was the County's only port and the courthouse was in Frederick, making the stretch of road connecting them extremely important.

By Monday, April 14, the troops reached Owens Ordinary, a tavern in the Hungerford section of old Rockville. The trip was an arduous one as the unseasonably warm weather took a turn for the worse with thunder, rain, and even snow that covered the soldiers' tents. After another sixteen-mile march, they camped on the hills near Clarksburg on April 15th. They had intended to be closer to Frederick, but a ferocious thunderstorm forced them to encamp at Dowden's Ordinary and spend the night. An eyewitness account describes the conditions they experienced:

> From sultry hot day it became excessively cold, and rained thunder and lightning till about 5 in the morning, when in 10 minutes it changed to snow, which in two hours covered the ground a foot and a half.
>
> The morning of April 16, they woke to a great quantity of snow…the snow being so violent we were oblig'd to beat it off the tents several times for fear it would Breck the tent Poles, reported a soldier. The weather prevented them from moving …on account of bad wether we halted to-day, though a terrible place, for we could neither get provisions for ourselves, nor fodder for our horses, and as it was wet in the camp it was very disagreeable, and no house to go into.

On April 17th, the weather cleared and they were able to continue their march toward Frederick on roads that were "very mountainous." They crossed the Monocacy River that night and were able to camp four miles south of Frederick. Braddock, who was traveling separately, arrived on April 21st.

One can only wonder at the bizarre weather the forces encountered. Hot and humid is quite common in April in Montgomery County, but snow? A portent of the tragedy to come? If only Braddock had heeded the warning signs or even the advice of his colonial allies…

Clarksburg, Md., Where Pres. Jackson Dined on Way to Inauguration

Dowden's Ordinary in Clarksburg, ca. 1900, where Braddock's troops weathered an unseasonable snowstorm. The building is no longer standing and this is now the site of an archaeological park.
Courtesy of Montgomery County Historical Society.

They finally joined up with the other regiment of soldiers at Wills Creek near Cumberland. There were about a hundred American Indians lodged near the fort who gaped at the red-coated strangers who gaped back. The area had come alive with soldiers, frontier volunteers, women, Indians, supply wagons, and guns. The officers had expected more fresh food, more Indians, indeed more of everything. In a compounding of disappointments and frustrations, they discovered that their biscuits were moldy and the meat musty.

At the urging of George Washington, one of Braddock's young officers, the General left half of his force at Cumberland to await supplies. On May 29, the first of Braddock's party headed northerly for Fort Duquesne (now Pittsburgh) to engage the French. The march was over rough, rocky, wooded terrain, land that had previously known no heavier tread than an Indian moccasin, or rarely, a frontiersman's or fur trader's boot. Now the land was jolted by the presence of 2,000 soldiers and all of their guns, mortars, horses, and wagons. Every inch of the way had to be won in a struggle with the steep hills and choking undergrowth. The men and animals, perilously undernourished, suffered from heat and fatigue. The French had won initial psychological advantage with spine-chilling stories of scalping Indians and burnings. The British regulars in their cumbersome uniforms were as out of place as the Indians would have been at Windsor Castle. General Braddock wrote to a friend that "we are sent like sacrifices to the altar." Never was a prophecy so painfully accurate.

In July, the expedition crossed a creek near the Monongahela River and was jubilant with success. The jubilation would not last long. When the British forces at last met the French, the terrain was perfect for an ambush. Braddock found his army in a newly created twelve foot wide roadway with steep slopes on either side. Braddock's troops were caught in that trench. The British regulars were used to the more orderly wheel-and-fire method of fighting. Being trapped in the trench threw them into confusion. The officers attempted to stem the panic, but the soldiers kept falling back, piling into the oncoming troops who did not realize the situation. The clustered and bright-colored red coats made a perfect target for the enemy of French soldiers and their Indian comrades. George Washington had two horses shot from under him and four musket balls through his coat, but otherwise was uninjured. Braddock had five horses shot from beneath him and then was fatally wounded himself. In the stinging smoke and utter disarray, the British regulars whirled in a kaleidoscope of death and retreat. The pursuing Indians had their scalps and the French had their victory. For the British it was a startling, humiliating, and deadly defeat, but for George Washington, it was the beginning of a legend.

To this day, General Braddock's army is said to march yet in the Potomac valley along River Road, in the low lying areas near Cabin John Creek. That was the last place where they had any feeling of comfort and safety. If you are in that area in the midnight hour, you may see something luminous and white. Don't be too hasty to dismiss it as a patch of fog drifting along the river. It may be a mist on your bifocals or it may be long-forgotten ghosts of the Potomac past. The local people living in that area spin yarns of a ghostly army said to materialize in the midnight hours along that low-lying stretch of road. They tell of hearing drumbeats, bugle calls, the tread of marching feet, the grinding of wheels, the rattle of trace chains, and the creaking of harnesses, which all fill the darkness as the spirit army marches as a vague gray form into the endless night of their ghostly existence. They are the disembodied marchers from another era. Legend also has it that a mysterious pale horse and rider sometimes appears and disappears, with its rider roaring out commands in a sepulchral voice. Could it be the ghost of Braddock himself?

To read more about the Braddock Campaign, we suggest the book *Braddock Road Chronicles 1755* by Andrew Wahll.

Chapter 20: Cabin John

Cabin John Bridge

BY ANONYMOUS

MacArthur Boulevard follows the course of the Potomac River, winding from Georgetown out to Great Falls, Maryland, through the towns of Glen Echo and Cabin John. Between these two towns, a massive stone archway carries the road high over the Cabin John Creek.

Soldiers march across the Cabin John Bridge, ca. 1865.
Source: Library of Congress.

Nowadays, the 150-yard, one-lane Cabin John Bridge has traffic lights at each end to control the flow of traffic and iron-work guardrails to protect pedestrians from said traffic. However, when my father grew up in Cabin John in the 1950s and 1960s, literally a stone's throw from the end of the bridge, traffic was two-way on narrow lanes, and pedestrians took their chances. Granted, traffic back then was much less than it is now; still, crossing the bridge could be a nerve-wracking experience.

During his grade school years, my father delivered the *Washington Post* every morning. Today the paper lands, maybe, on your driveway in a plastic bag hurled from a passing car. My father walked his route, putting the papers on the doorsteps or, in bad weather, behind the screen door. He went out at four in the morning when there was no traffic. In good weather, you could see the morning constellations. The best place to see the stars, far away from the street lights and trees, was from the center of the bridge.

The Cabin John Bridge, shown here in 1915, used to have two-way traffic.
Source: Library of Congress.

At least, that was the reason my father gave for standing in the middle of the Cabin John Bridge one fine spring morning in 1964, when he was thirteen. Over time, another reason has surfaced, one that better explains his reticence in telling the tale at the time of its occurrence.

He was, indeed, out on the bridge after delivering the papers, but he wasn't stargazing — he was throwing glass Coke bottles off the bridge into the creek below. He was also listening for the occasional car or delivery truck, since getting caught was not on the list of things to do that morning. What he heard, though, was a sound new to him, a rhythmic sound, as if someone — many "someones" — was marching.

This, of course, made no sense. Who would be marching at four o'clock in the morning? On MacArthur Boulevard? He peered down the road toward Glen Echo, but the curve of the road limited his view. He stood there in the middle of the bridge, puzzling, until he suddenly realized they were coming his way! Right now! He turned on his heel, ran the half-bridge-length back to the Cabin John side, dove into the runoff ditch by the side of the road, and hunkered down, out of sight. He listened as the marching neared the bridge, and then he heard a command that he didn't understand at the time: "Break step, march." The footsteps changed from marching cadence to plain walking as the soldiers came across the bridge. Not until years later, when he was in the service himself, did he learn that a company of soldiers doesn't march, in unison, across a bridge; the marching rhythm can create vibrations that might damage the structure.

At the time, my father only knew that people were walking across the bridge and right past where he was huddled at the bottom of the ditch. (Kids at night, even paperboys, just don't like being seen.) He heard the footsteps, the clothing rustling, and the clanking of metal on metal. It seemed like hundreds of men trooped by before they were finally off the bridge. He heard the command, "Resume step, march." In three beats, the rhythm of the footsteps went from walking to marching. When they were finally all past, curiosity overcame fear and my father crawled up the side of the ditch and looked after them, up the road toward Cabin John. It was a clear night. The roadway, on the Cabin John side of the bridge, runs in a straight line for nearly a mile — and it was empty.

My father listened to the marching footsteps until they were out of earshot, and then he slid back down into the ditch and stayed there until the sun was high in the sky.

To read more on the Washington Aqueduct, we suggest the book *The Washington Aqueduct 1952-1992* by Harry Ways.

Postscript: The Cabin John Bridge is not just a bridge, it is also an aqueduct. Beneath the road surface is the large, nine-foot pipe that supplies water to Washington, D.C. When it was built, the bridge was the longest single-span stone arch in the world. The Cabin John Bridge — originally known as the Union Arch — was built just before the Civil War, and there was concern that the Confederates might try to disrupt the capital's water supply. The Union Army set patrols to prevent damage or sabotage, and the Union Arch survived the war intact. Perhaps this particular troop of soldiers never got the word that the aqueduct was no longer in danger.

Chapter 21: Chevy Chase

Rossdhu Castle Gatehouse

BY DOROTHY PUGH

Once upon a time there was a castle in Chevy Chase, perched high on a hill overlooking Rock Creek Park. Rossdhu came complete with turrets, battlements, and thirty rooms. It even had a gatehouse with its own turrets that guarded the curving drive up the hill to the castle. In front of it was the Chevy Chase version of a moat — call it a pond — otherwise known as "Wee Loch Lomond." This castle complex was a dream come true for Clarence Crittenden Calhoun, a Kentucky lawyer, and his wife, Daisy Donovan O'Donovan Breaux Simonds Gummere Calhoun, an artistic and literary society matron who hobnobbed with presidents and royalty when she could.

Interesting as the castle was, it couldn't hold a candle to Daisy. Born Margaret Rose Anthony Julia Josephine Catherine Cornelia Donovan O'Donovan in St. Louis, Missouri, she was the daughter of Cornelius MacCarthy Moore Donovan O'Donovan. When he died, her mother, Josephine Marr, married a prominent lawyer in Louisiana, Gustav A. Breaux, and Daisy took his name. She became a belle of New Orleans and, when she was eighteen years old, she married Andrew Calhoun Simonds, a banker in Charleston, South Carolina. He built the Villa Margherita (Italian for Daisy) for her on the Charleston waterfront. The Villa enabled Daisy to come into her own as a hostess, entertaining in her home three presidents: Grover Cleveland, Theodore Roosevelt, and William Howard Taft.

When Andy Simons died, Daisy moved north and married another banker, Barker Gummere of Princeton, New Jersey. He provided her with a mansion named Rosedale House, charmingly placed in a seventeen-acre park. This time she attracted a future United States president, Woodrow Wilson, who was then the head of Princeton University. He attended Rosedale's housewarming along with Henry Van Dyke, who wrote a poem for the occasion.

Rossdhu Gatehouse and Castle. Rossdhu Castle was torn down in 1957.
Castle image courtesy Chevy Chase Historical Society.

Life should have been good for Daisy, but unfortunately her second husband also died. She gathered up her daughter, Margaret, and headed for Washington, D.C., perhaps because World War I was raging and she felt safer living near a president she had entertained. Woodrow Wilson was now leading the country. She threw her considerable artistic talents into wartime charitable work, writing a patriotic play in which she starred along with her future husband, Clarence Calhoun. Clarence had won fame by winning Kentucky's lawsuit against the Federal government for its post-Civil War claims. He had also won ownership of the Black Hills of South Dakota for the Sioux Indian Tribe. They were so appreciative that they made him a member of the tribe.

Soon after Daisy and Clarence were married, the romantic, young Edward, Prince of Wales, came to town and met Daisy's daughter, Margaret. When he asked to visit Margaret, Daisy achieved her greatest hostess triumph by entertaining royalty. Not to be outdone, Clarence greeted the Prince dressed as a Sioux chief while giving authentic Indian war whoops. The record fails to show if Edward ever visited again at the Calhouns. He did go on to become King Edward VIII of England and then abdicated the throne so he could marry a Baltimore belle, twice-divorced Wallis Warfield Simpson. They finished their days as the Duke and Duchess of Windsor.

That royal visit may have planted the idea of living in a castle in the minds of Daisy and Clarence. According to one account, they both claimed descent from the fabled Scottish king, Robert the Bruce. Clarence descended down through the Calhouns, whose ancestral home was an early castle called Rossdhu, home of the "Clan Coquhoun on Loch Lomond. When Daisy and Clarence informed Sir Ian Calhoun, patriarch of the clan, that they were building their own Rossdhu Castle, he sent a capstone from a tower of the old Rossdhu to be set over the lintel of the new Rossdhu's front door. Another Scottish stone, this one from the eleventh century castle of Robert the Bruce, serves as the keystone of the large fireplace in the gatehouse.

The Grand Opening of Rossdhu Castle was held on New Year's Eve 1927. The finished castle had round and square turrets, battlements on all the upper levels, thirty rooms, and of course the requisite ballroom, featuring a marble floor measuring thirty by forty feet. Daisy called the substantial gatehouse at the bottom of the hill Braemar Lodge, a tribute to her other ancestors, the Earls of Mar, who had owned Braemar Castle in Scotland. (Interestingly, that castle is now owned by the Farquharson clan, progenitors of the local Farquhars. (See "Olney House," Chapter 4.) The surrounding Chevy Chase area was known as Braemar Forest.

Unfortunately, Daisy and Clarence had barely finished furnishing their new home when the stock market crashed in 1929, leaving them without the means to sustain life in a fairytale castle. They retreated to the gatehouse and turned the castle into a posh nightclub, trying to make a pitcher of lemonade out of a huge lemon, but times were just too bad and the Calhouns couldn't hold onto their dream.

In 1934, the castle was auctioned off and broken up into apartments with the marble-floored ballroom becoming the lobby of the building. A *Washington Star* article by Dick Wright in 1975 depicted the castle as a sort of swinging singles pad — and not just for humans. One of the tenants found a young red fox in the woods and tamed and raised it. It found life at the wild castle to be much more fun than life in the wild outdoors.

The shenanigans didn't bother the middle-aged caretaker who liked a little revelry himself. One night when his partying became a little too raucous, the gatehouse residents felt compelled to call the police. When the gendarmes arrived, the caretaker stumbled out, carrying a .22 caliber rifle in one hand and a fifth of liquor in the other. Strangely enough, the astonished comment from a police officer was, "Am I seeing things or is that a damn fox sitting there in the doorway?

There was also the very warm evening when two bachelor tenants, sans clothes, couldn't resist the cooling depths of the moat/pond. One hopes the police allowed them to dress before trotting them off to their own cooler.

Captain Calhoun, builder of the castle, died in 1938. Daisy continued to live in part of the gatehouse until moving to Charleston, South Carolina, where she died eleven years after Clarence.

While living in Maryland, Daisy had been involved in political, social, cultural, and literary activities, even penning some poetry:

> If life is not as you would make it,
> You can, at least, show how to take it;
> If you must 'take it on the chin,'
> Then learn to take it with a grin;
> For, if you keep on 'Smilin Thru'
> Life's Mirror will smile back at you.

One wonders if that is how she got through the loss of three husbands and her beloved castle. What a woman!

The castle suffered another blow after World War II. The area was re-zoned and only single-family dwellings were allowed — no more apartments, no more high-jinks. On August 26, 1957, a wrecking ball demolished the walls, effectively erasing Rossdhu Castle from its hill.

Unlike the castle, the substantial guardian gatehouse managed to survive, nestled neatly in what remained of the property. In 1939, after Clarence Calhoun had died, the gatehouse was purchased by Bert Williams, who had managed the castle apartments at one time. After Daisy moved back to Charleston, the Williams' occupied the entire gatehouse and had a ball filling their little castle with antiques. This was easily done, as they were longtime owners of a Connecticut Avenue shop near Chevy Chase Lake which they called "Grandma's Antiques." (During World War II the Williams' also owned the well-known inn and restaurant, "Hilltop House," in Harper's Ferry.)

Bert and his wife enjoyed their gatehouse castle for many years, but in the summer of 1974, poor Bert fell dead — right on the gatehouse doorstep. Today there are signs that Bert didn't want to leave, and is still wandering through his beloved little castle.

Mrs. Williams put the house on the market, and the building passed through several owners and some necessary renovations, until Jeanne Broulik discovered it was once again for sale. When younger, Jeanne had often ridden her horse through the woods around the big castle and fantasized about living there, never dreaming that someday she would actually own the little castle.

Jeanne and her husband, Frank, bought the charming, crenellated building in 1979. Jeanne loved her little castle gatehouse, considering it "very romantic," and came to feel that perhaps she had been destined to live there. She felt many connections to it: like Clarence Calhoun, her husband, Frank, was a captain; her son was born in Charleston, where Daisy had built her Villa Margherita; her daughter lived in Princeton, New Jersey, where Daisy's Rosedale Mansion still stood; and Jeanne also wrote poetry, just as Daisy had… It was all a little eerie perhaps.

It didn't take long for Jeanne to feel that she and Frank weren't alone in the gatehouse. She said that she didn't believe in ghosts, but felt the gatehouse definitely was haunted. She could find no other explanation for the front door periodically slamming with no wind or push from anyone. From anyone alive, that is! She suspected that Bert Williams, who had died on the gatehouse doorstep, was still trying to make it inside to say his last good-byes. He seems to be quite persistent, as the slamming is still being heard.

Jeanne's son, Jan Broulik, the present owner, once stood inside the entryway and actually saw the door open and close. Another time, Jan was painting a pillar in the hall down from the front door when he sensed a movement. He turned to look and saw a man standing there in that small entryway dressed in working clothes — a man who immediately disappeared. Suddenly there was no one there. But Jan knew he hadn't imagined it.

Joe Phillips, who also lives in the gatehouse, has had reports from his mother, Betty, that when she stayed there on the ground floor, she often heard mysterious footsteps going up the spiral stairs of the round tower in the middle of the night.

Jeanne Broulik herself died in the gatehouse, but upstairs in her bed in the front bedroom. For three days after, her son, Jan, felt her presence watching over him. Then she evidently knew he would be all right, and she went on to wherever spirits go when they move on.

After Jeanne's death, her husband, Frank, stayed on in the house and is responsible, along with Jan, for the current interesting and attractive areas outside the little castle. The original driveway through the gatehouse is now a colorful, tiled courtyard adorned with urns, flowers, and even benches from Daisy's Charleston Villa Margherita. It still overlooks the moat/pond, now smaller in size, but sporting a lovely fountain and an interesting array of ducks plus a pair of geese in season.

When Frank Broulik fell dead of a heart attack in the living room, it was almost directly beneath where Jeanne had died. Jan Broulik used an Ouija board to stay in touch with his father. When Jan would ask questions, Frank would reply. Once Frank's sister was coming to visit and Frank expressly asked Jan not to have her stay in the house, but she did. Sure enough, she managed to break the plumbing in a second floor bathroom and water poured down through the living room ceiling near where Frank had died! She's never been asked back! Strangely, though, when the floor/ceiling was being repaired, Frank's old, initialed tape measure was found where he had accidentally left it years before during a previous repair. Was this all a plan?

Through the years there have been other unexplained phenomena such as the two golden lights that first appeared at the back of the courtyard. They were round balls the size of oranges. Jan could find no explanation for them. Another time they appeared over the pond, where one followed the other to the end and disappeared in the distance. Again, no explanation…

Two siblings who lived in the house as children occasionally visit and nowadays they always hear a woman singing when they do come. Could it be Jeanne Broulik who died in the house? The music seems to be from the 1930s, though, so it's more likely that it's Daisy, who went through such a traumatic time in those years. She may be remembering her great architectural triumph here, and wants to hang around because she had such a short time in which to savor it!

Soldiers in the Well

BY DOROTHY PUGH

In the early 1970s, there was a lovely old farmhouse on Turner Lane in Chevy Chase. Its expansive backyard displayed a beautiful rose garden. There was also a fountain flowing into a fish pond. In the middle of the yard was a charming old well, safely bricked over and covered with growing ivy. These grounds were carefully kept up by a very talented gardener, an immigrant who had escaped from Hungary during the 1956 uprising against the Soviets.

Alexis Lang, a teenager who lived next-door, often enjoyed the view of this enchanting garden from her upstairs bedroom window. One warm summer evening she was looking out and saw a filmy, translucent figure walking from the well to the house. She couldn't believe her eyes. It was very strange. The figure faded away, but then she heard eerie noises. She heard someone counting down from ten to one. When it first happened, she called her father upstairs, and he heard the noises, too. Even Johann, the Hungarian gardener, said he had heard them.

Alexis continued to see filmy figures near that old well. When she told neighbors about it, she learned about the bodies of three Union soldiers that had been dumped in that well. They were supposedly Civil War soldiers who had been killed in the skirmishing near the Battle of Fort Stevens in the District of Columbia. Turner Lane is only a short distance from D.C.

In those hot, dusty Civil War days of early July 1864, General Jubal Early's troops were charging through Maryland, hoping to capture Washington, D.C. for the Confederates. Right then the city was a fat plum ripe for the picking. It contained very few defenders, but the heat and fatigue delayed Early's men; as a result, by July 12th, when they finally attacked Fort Stevens, General Grant had managed to shore up its defenses with some seasoned Union men. Washington was saved, though bullets were flying and men were dying all over the area, so perhaps it isn't so strange that three Union soldiers ended up in a well in Chevy Chase. As Joseph Judge wrote about that battle in his book *Season of Fire*, "The dead sleep in many places."

To read more about the raid on Washington, we suggest *Season of Fire: The Confederate Strike on Washington* by Joseph Judge.

Chapter 22: Glen Echo

Glen Echo Carousel

BY ANONYMOUS

The Glen Echo Amusement Park opened in 1911; its heyday was the 1930s and 1940s. One of the most popular attractions was the Dentzel carousel, or merry-go-round, built in 1921. The amusement park closed in 1968, but today the carousel, restored to its former glory, is the centerpiece of the National Park Service's Glen Echo Park.

This ghost story is about that carousel. I believe this story because I know the person it happened to, way back in 1965, when my friend was thirteen years old. He says he saw the ghosts twice. The first time, he saw them by accident. The second time, he saw them on purpose. He hasn't been back a third time, and it's been more than forty years now.

My friend never told anybody about the ghosts until just a few years ago, and when I asked him why not, he pointed out that you can only see the ghosts at night, when the park is closed. I said, "Yeah, so?" He said he was supposed to be at home, in bed, asleep, and not in the park at midnight. So, you see, he couldn't very well tell anybody about the ghosts, could he?

Still, when he was thirteen, he liked to sneak out at night. He especially liked to sneak into Glen Echo Park after it was closed for the day. He would walk around and look at the rides or sit on the picnic tables and look for tickets that someone might have dropped. (He never did find any, he says.) Each time that he went to the park, he'd sneak in and stay in the shadows until he was pretty sure that no one else was there. If he wasn't sure, he'd just sneak back out and return another time.

Full view of the Dentzel Carousel at Glen Echo Park and the Carousel horses. The Carousel was built in 1921.

The carousel, closed up at night, didn't look like much. It was just a round building with big folding doors and lots of windows in the doors. Certainly, nothing too interesting to a thirteen-year-old, but one time, when he was hiding in the shadows, being extra careful because of the moonlight (he doesn't know if the moon was full or not, but it was pretty bright), he thought he saw shadows moving on the doors of the carousel. He looked around, trying to figure out what was making the shadows, but he didn't see anything else moving in the park. He started edging toward the carousel, making sure to stay out of sight. As he got closer, he could hear the music of the calliope through the closed doors. When he got right up to the carousel and looked in the windows, he could see the moonlight flashing off the brass poles as they went by and the animals in the middle going up and down. The merry-go-round was turning — and there were people riding on it. They were African American and they were all dressed up in their Sunday-best. My friend stared at them, watching them go around, all smiles. Confused, he wondered how all these people got into the park and why in the world they were there in the middle of the night. Just then a cloud covered the moon for a moment and, when the moonlight came back, the carousel was empty.

My friend says that he backed away from that carousel so fast he tripped over himself and fell on his butt. He got up, raced through the park, climbed over the fence — which was about ten feet tall — and took off across the parking lot as fast as he could. He ran all the way home, which was about a mile. You also have to remember that this was long before they invented running shoes (a "mile" was a whole lot longer back then!).

Anyway, during that summer, he went back to the amusement park several more times, but he never saw anything, so he gave up. However, one night in the fall, after the park was closed for the season, he snuck back in again. It was nearly full moon again, with no clouds, and as soon as he got to where he could see the carousel, he knew it was moving. He could just barely hear the music, and he could see the shadows. He watched it for a long time before he got up the nerve to sneak closer and look in. Just as before, there were families of African Americans, dressed up in their good clothes, riding the merry-go-round. There were children on the animals that went up and down, and parents standing next to the littlest kids, and old people in the chariots, everyone clearly having a good time riding the carousel. This time, my friend noticed that all of them — men and boys, women and girls — were wearing hats and old-fashioned-looking clothes, like you would see in the old black-and-white movies from the 1940s.

One of the men on the carousel glanced out the window at my friend and smiled. Spooked, my friend fell over backwards again as he tried to get away from the carousel. He ran just as fast as the first time and climbed the fence and took off across the parking lot, although this time, he said, he only managed to run about half the way home.

After that, my friend still snuck out of his house at night (of course), but he never did go back into the park when it was closed — and he still won't.

In the mid-1960s, when the incidents in this story took place, Glen Echo Amusement Park had only been integrated for a few years. For most of its history, Glen Echo and its amusements was open to whites only. African Americans from the District and from Cabin John could only look in from the edges and wonder what it might be like to enjoy the rides in the park. The 1961 season was the first time the park was open to all, and tensions between African American guests and some of the white employees remained a problem for several years.

The park's segregation gives us a hint as to the origins of this haunting, but the full story is unknown. Are the ghostly carousel riders enjoying some kind of spiritual wish-fulfillment? Or were there in fact occasions in the 1940s when some unknown person opened the park at night for those people who couldn't come in during the day? Unless someone else comes forward with more stories or information about the haunted carousel, we may never know.

To read more about Glen Echo Park, we suggest *Glen Echo Park: A Story of Survival* by Richard Cooke and Deborah Lange.

ROCK CREEK

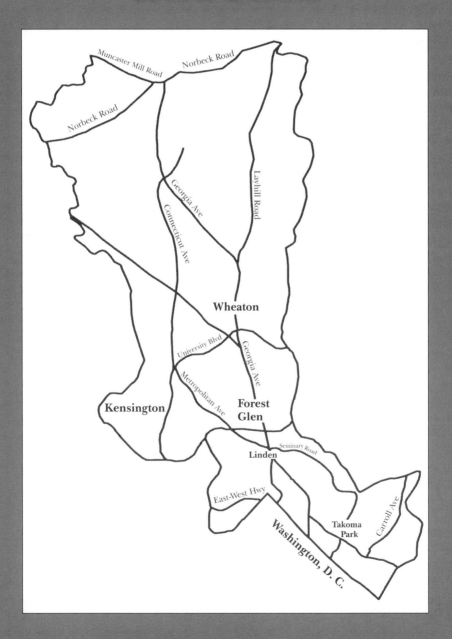

Chapter 23: Forest Glen

National Park Seminary

FROM BARBARA FINCH

Montgomery County is home to what is probably one of the most architecturally unusual communities in the country. For those who have passed this hidden gem, the first response is usually, "What is that?!" Ye Forest Inn opened in 1887 as a summer resort, but it didn't take long for the owners to realize it wasn't going to be an economic success. By 1894, the resort had become National Park Seminary, an elite girls' school attracting East Coast society's future leading lights. John and Vesta Cassedy had a vision of creating a school that not only educated their charges, but also inspired them. To that end, they filled their school with whimsical buildings that illustrated iconic architectural styles — the Japanese Pagoda, the Greek Pantheon, the French Chateau, the Dutch Windmill, etc. — as well as classical sculpture in a bucolic setting designed for contemplation. After Vesta died, Dr. Cassedy sold the school to Dr. James Eli Ament, who ran it for twenty years. When he died, his widow turned it over to Dr. Roy Tasco Davis. All were renowned educators.

The school had trouble during the depression, but it was still there when World War II began. Then in 1942 Dr. Davis made the mistake of inviting some important military men to have dinner at the school. They immediately saw that it would make an excellent rehabilitation and convalescent center for wounded soldiers released from Walter Reed Army Hospital, which was not far away. The War Powers Act was invoked, and the girls' school became the Walter Reed Army Hospital Forest Glen Annex. Physically and emotionally injured WW II veterans were brought to rest and receive treatment at the beautiful, rural property.

One of the highlights of the Seminary was the ballroom. This beautiful building had a soaring ceiling, Gothic-style arches, and balconies overlooking the dance floor. In addition to the rehab activities, soldiers could look forward to dances and other social events with local girls.

The Seminary was actively used by the Army through the end of the Vietnam War, but by the 1980s, its use as a medical annex was unnecessary and the buildings fell into disrepair. A friend and I had heard ghost stories about the dilapidated property and went to investigate one day.

Ballroom at the National Park Seminary, 1936.
Source: HABS, Library of Congress.

After a while, we came across a man and woman and chatted with them about the beauty of the buildings and grounds, expressing concerns that the buildings might never be renovated. My friend and I also mentioned hearing about ghosts. The man said he didn't believe in ghosts, but, as we chatted some more, he paused and, rather grudgingly, told us an amazing story.

He said that in the 1960s the Army sponsored dances in the ballroom a few times each year. He told us he attended a Valentine's Day dance there one night. At one point the man happened to look up and saw several servicemen in uniform in the balconies looking down upon the dance. He said that they looked rather sad, as though they were envious of the young people who were dancing and having fun. A little later he looked up again and noticed that the men's hairstyles and uniforms were not of the 1960s, but rather World War II. He then realized that they were not completely solid — he could see through them and knew they must be ghosts.

The man was uncomfortable as he recounted the story, as if he didn't want us to think he was crazy. We were delighted to hear his story and wished we had been at the dance and seen the ghosts, too!

Thankfully, the property is in the process of restoration. As ghosts often are disturbed when a building is undergoing renovation, I wonder if any of the workers are experiencing a haunting. So far I haven't heard any stories to that effect.

To read more about the National Park Seminary, we suggest *Enchanted Forest Glen: The Endangered Legacy of National Park Seminary Historic District in Silver Spring , MD* by Halper Lee and Jane Freundel Levey and *Forest Glen* by Rich Schaffer and Ric Nelson.

Chapter 24: Four Corners

Haunting Music

FROM BARBARA FINCH

Many years ago, I met two graduate students who were sharing a house with a third housemate. The house is an old Cape Cod-style from the 1940s and is located on Dryden Street in the Four Corners area of Silver Spring. We became friendly and one night they invited me and my friends to their house for dinner. After dinner, we were laughing and having a good time… It was during a pause in the conversation when we all heard a noise from down in the basement, which did not have a door. It sounded as though someone had banged a hard object.

Immediately the two students who lived there stiffened up, glanced at each other, and looked uncomfortable. "What was that?" I asked. They didn't reply. My friends and I looked at them and asked again. Finally they told us that they had experienced several unnerving incidents and were convinced the house was haunted. Of course, my friends and I were excited to hear more and pressed them for details.

All three housemates were musicians and had several musical instruments in the house. A drum set was in the basement, and they said they had heard someone down there banging on the drums from time to time — when no one was down there.

Their housemate had a harpsichord in the living room, and several times at night they heard someone pressing the keys playfully as a child might. Whenever they went to investigate, nobody was there.

Finally, they said that fairly regularly — when only one person was at home and in his or her room — they would hear the front door open and then the footsteps of someone walking through the living room and going up the stairs to the second floor. They became very uncomfortable with it and finally reached the point that they would just stay in their rooms until another housemate came home.

Sometime later I needed a new place to live, and they told me that their third housemate was moving out. They reminded me about the ghost, but I was determined not to be bothered. When we moved in my possessions, I walked into the house, clapped loudly, and addressed the spirit. I said that I was moving in and that we no longer wanted him/her to bother us. I also said that it was time for him/her to move on and that he/she was no longer welcome there. We never had another problem, and the house felt quite clean.

Chapter 25: Silver Spring

The Ghost Who Laughed Last

FROM BARBARA FINCH

Many years ago, a friend of mine who lived on Thayer Avenue in Silver Spring suffered a long illness. When no more could be done for him at the hospital, he came home to die.

He had a posse of friends and volunteers who came to help with his care. Additionally, a nurse came to check on him periodically. Unfortunately, she did not approve of my friend's lifestyle and his associates. My friend could not speak by that time, and they would just glare at each other. It was a very strange contrast as otherwise the house was filled with loving people who did everything they could to make my friend comfortable during his transition.

After he passed, I stayed at the house for a few days. When I got there after work in the evenings, I would hear a soft "Hi," which was how my friend had always greeted me when I came over. It was a nice reminder that he wasn't really dead, just no longer in physical form.

A couple of days later the nurse phoned and said she needed to come and pick up some medical equipment her agency had lent us. When she came, I offered to help, but she declined. I held the door open for her and tried to make small talk with her, but she wasn't interested.

After a couple of minutes, she appeared noticeably anxious. Each time she brought equipment out of the bedroom (where my friend had passed), she walked faster and faster. I trailed after her, asking if everything was okay, but she didn't answer. She just looked very frightened. Finally, she made her last trip from the bedroom. I asked if that was all, and she blurted a "Yes" as she ran out. She jumped into her car and spun gravel as she peeled out of the driveway and took off down the street!

I stood there at the door with my mouth hanging open, completely mystified by her behavior, and then I clearly heard my friend laughing! I suddenly realized he must have made his presence known to her — maybe a little harmless revenge?

Linden House

FROM MARGARET WILLIAMS

Jim and Mary and their eight children had outgrown their house in Cabin John Gardens. After looking for another home for years, they finally found a three-story Victorian house in the Linden neighborhood of Silver Spring. The price of the house was much higher than they expected, and they had to think about whether they could afford it. They asked the owner, a widow, if they could think about it over the weekend. Against her realtor's advice, the widow took the house off the market until Jim and Mary made their decision. Of course they purchased the home and became fast friends with the widow.

Now that the house of their dreams was theirs, Jim and Mary had no money to hire a mover, so they decided to carry out the move on their own. They rented a truck and shuttled the truck between the two houses, filling the new house with their lives, but a family of ten requires a lot of stuff for living so the move was not finished by the evening of the first day. With only part of the house furnished, it was decided that Mary and the younger children would stay in the new house that night, and the older children would stay with Jim in the old home.

Mary settled all of the children in their new bedrooms and, after securing the house, went to sleep. She was awakened in the night by a man standing in the doorway of her room. In her drowsy state, she could only vaguely see him and, thinking that he was one of her older sons, Mary was unruffled as she asked if he needed anything. When he didn't answer, she turned the light on and turning back to the door, found him gone. Mary got up, checked the house, and found everything still locked up tightly and undisturbed. So, after checking on the children, she went back to bed.

The next morning, while trying to fix breakfast in a new unpacked house, Mary barely responded when the younger children asked about the man who had come into their rooms the previous night. None of the children were frightened, but they hadn't recognized him. Mary finally realized that it wasn't her son, but someone else in her new home. Since they knew that she had checked all the doors and that the house had remained locked, the children decided that their new house had a ghost — someone that could walk through walls. They told the older children all about it when they arrived at the new house with the first load for the day. The skeptical older children pooh-poohed the idea and decided that the widow must have a friend with a key who came in, but left when he didn't recognize the residents. After changing the locks and settling into their new home, that is how the family left it.

They forgot about the strange man until Mary visited the widow a few busy months later. They were having tea in the widow's living room when Mary noticed a picture of the widow and a few friends. There in the picture was the man in her doorway that first night in the home. Mary told the widow the humorous story of the man coming into the house and finding new people. She hoped that he was able to contact the widow since he never came by the house again. The widow grew very quiet and told Mary that the man was her husband and that he had died five years before she put the house on the market.

Surprise turned to wonder as they both decided that the widow's husband was checking out the new residents. Having approved of them, he felt no need to return. The widow felt that her husband contacted her to show his approval and love. Mary felt that with the ghostly visit, the house was blessed and continued to be the entire time she lived there with her large family. When Jim and Mary's oldest daughter purchased the house from her parents, she also felt the blessings and approval in the home — and I feel it to this day!

Postscript: I was one of the skeptical older children on that fateful moving day. I came in at breakfast and scoffed at the story concocted by my brothers and sisters. I remained incredulous until the day that I went with my mother to visit the widow, Polly Zens, and saw first-hand their reaction to the news of William Zens' ghostly visit. Our ghost never returned, but the house still retains that wonderful, welcoming feel and retains the blessings that love gives.

Chapter 26: Woodside

The Bridesmaid

BY DOROTHY PUGH

It was on one spring evening back in the early part of the twentieth century that Frank Willson married Linda Waters at her family home in Woodside. With family members and friends in attendance, the rector of Grace Episcopal Church officiated the ceremony. Afterwards, a joyful reception got under way with soft candlelight providing the ambience for the celebration. Unfortunately, the bride ventured too close to one of the candles and her veil caught fire. A guest immediately tore it from her head and the flames were quickly stomped out. However, a bridesmaid was standing nearby and her dress caught fire. She was engulfed in flames and, although several male guests wrapped their coats around her, she was badly burned. Sixteen-year-old Elizabeth Earl Willson, only sister of the groom, died two days later at her parents' home near Layhill.

Years later people who lived in the house where the fire occurred started getting strange sensations. They didn't feel that they were the only ones living in the house, so they called in a psychic. After wandering through the rooms, the psychic said there definitely was a ghost. She felt a chilly wind, especially in the dining room — the room where the tragic reception had taken place.

Strangely, the owners were also awakened in the night by the smell of coffee brewing. Could the chill have been too much for the ghost, too, who felt the need of a warm liquid? Selfishly the spirit only shared the aroma; the owners still had to brew their own morning coffee.

EASTERN COUNTY

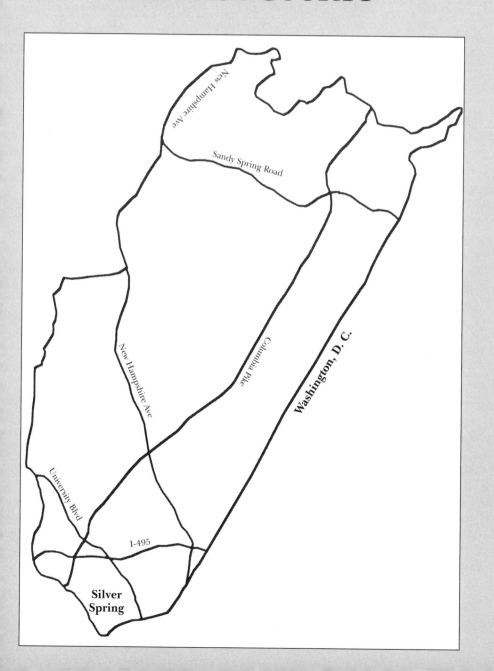

Chapter 27:
Silver Spring – East

Blair Mansion

BY
DOROTHY
PUGH

Blair Mansion stands on land that remained in one family for more than two hundred years, 1685 until after 1900. The original grant, Girl's Portion, was given to George Pierce by King Charles II of England. Some two hundred years later, Abner Shoemaker, a member of the Pierce family, gave a portion of that land to his niece, Abigail, who was engaged to Charles Rider Newman. Generous Abner also gave them a fine large mansion designed by the well-known architect Stanford White. In his career, White designed many famous structures, including the Washington Square Arch and the second Madison Square Garden in New York City, so getting him to design Blair Mansion was quite a plum. Uncle Abner also imported more than $100,000 worth of furnishings from France for the young couple. What a start in life they had!

However, the groom, Charles Newman, had an unfortunate gambling habit and, within ten years, had lost everything. As a result, the property was sold at a tax auction.

The building went through several owners and incarnations. Besides being a tea house and guest house at one time, it has hosted many important social and political gatherings. At one time it was an outpost for recovering soldiers from nearby Walter Reed Hospital. Eventually it settled down as a restaurant, now owned by the Zeender brothers — Robert, Roger, and Ramon. They had the building extensively renovated, returning it to its original 1880s appearance. They serve varied and interesting food in their dining rooms and also have seven other rooms available for private parties. On weekends they offer an interactive murder mystery in one of the rooms, along with a delicious meal. Some recent titles are: "A Murderous Matrimony," "Murder Bytes," and "Which Blair Project?"

We don't know what sweet, young Abigail did when forced to abandon her stylish new mansion, but we think we know what she's doing now. She seems to be clattering through the halls of Blair Mansion Restaurant, switching lights on and off, moving things, knocking things off walls, trying to be the mistress of the house again. She even manages to activate the door chimes which are controlled by a motion sensor.

One Sunday night a musician was sent upstairs to turn the lights off as the restaurant was closing. He had to leave them on in one room because a cleaning lady was working there with her bucket and broom. He came back down and reported to the manager, who said there were never any cleaning personnel there on a Sunday. Absolutely not! Hearing this, the musician "went bananas," realizing that he had seen a ghost. We doubt he ever played the restaurant again.

Blair Mansion, now a restaurant and mystery theater.
Courtesy Zeender Family.

We wonder, though, what Abigail was doing with a bucket and broom. Is she so particular about her old home that she herself would stoop to cleaning it if it didn't meet her exacting standards? We do know that she wants to assert her claim to the mansion. After a plaque with the Zeender family crest on it was discovered, it was proudly hung on a wall in the barroom above a lovely painting of the Zeender family castle in Switzerland. Abigail must have been incensed to find someone else's family name taking over *her* home! One day she couldn't take it anymore and, pulling both things from the wall, slammed them onto the floor while a manager and Robert watched! She was declaring that it was still *her* house!

Usually, Abigail gets along well with the Zeenders, who seem to enjoy having her around playing her tricks. They like to feel that they know her, and that she is pleased and proud to see her old house in such good condition and giving pleasure to so many of their patrons. She must also be glad that some of her possessions are being displayed in her old mansion, among them a three-tiered silver plate holder and a pair of shoes. We can also hope that she is pleased with the mystery theater. It seems very appropriate for a building housing a ghost.

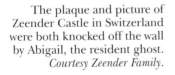

The plaque and picture of Zeender Castle in Switzerland were both knocked off the wall by Abigail, the resident ghost.
Courtesy Zeender Family.

Places to Visit

Most of the places mentioned in this book are private property. However, a number of them are museums, public parks and facilities which are available to visit and tour. Please contact the sites before visiting to determine hours and admission.

BALL'S BLUFF

On a bluff overlooking the Potomac River in Loudon County, Virginia, is the site of the Battle of Ball's Bluff and the National Cemetery. For more information, go to www.nps.gov/nr/travel/journey/bnc.htm. Also open to visitors is the Ball's Bluff Regional Battlefield located on Ball's Bluff Road. For more information go to www.nvrpa.org/park/ballsbluff.

BEALL-DAWSON HISTORICAL PARK

Address: 111 W. Montgomery Avenue, Rockville, Maryland 20850
Phone: 301-762-1492
Website: www.montgomeryhistory.org
This historic house museum explores county life in the nineteenth century. Also available for a tour in the park is the Stonestreet Museum of Nineteenth Century Medicine.

BLAIR MANSION

Address: 7711 Eastern Avenue, Silver Spring, Maryland 20912
Phone: 301-588-1688
Website: www.blairmansion.com
Blair Mansion is now a restaurant and dinner theater.

TOWN OF BROOKEVILLE

While the ghosts in Brookeville that are discussed in this book all reside in private homes, the Town of Brookeville has not changed much since Madison stayed there. A walking tour of historic Brookeville is available on their website at http://townofbrookevillemd.org/wt.html.

CHESAPEAKE & OHIO (C & O) CANAL NATIONAL HISTORICAL PARK

This 184-1/2-mile park stretches from Georgetown in Washington, D.C., to Cumberland, Maryland, with many access points along the way. The entrance to Great Falls and the Great Falls Tavern Visitor Center is located at 11710 MacArthur Boulevard (at the intersection of Falls Road), Potomac, Maryland 20854. For more information on the C & O Canal, go to www.nps.gov/choh.

GLEN ECHO PARK

Address: 7300 MacArthur Boulevard, Glen Echo, Maryland 20812
Phone: 301-634-2222
Website: www.glenechopark.org
This national historic site is home to a vibrant arts community, including artist's studios, Adventure Theatre, The Puppet Company, and of course the Dentzel Carousel (open May-September).

GLENVIEW MANSION/ROCKVILLE CIVIC CENTER PARK

Address: 603 Edmonston Drive, Rockville, Maryland 20850
Phone: 240-314-8660
Website: www.rockvillemd.gov/glenview
This nineteenth century home is now an art gallery and event facility for the City of Rockville.

LITTLE BENNETT REGIONAL PARK

Address: 23701 Frederick Road, Clarksburg, Maryland 20871
Phone: 301-528-3450
Website: www.montgomeryparks.org/facilities/regional_parks/little_
    bennett/index.shtm/
The nature center mentioned in the story is now the Hawk's Reach Activity Center.

OLNEY HOUSE

Address: 3308 Olney-Sandy Spring Road, Olney, Maryland 20832
Phone: 301-570-3388
Website: www.ricciutis.com
Olney House is now Ricciuti's Restaurant. While it has been renovated to serve its current purpose, many of the original features can be seen.

OLNEY THEATRE

Address: 2001 Olney-Sandy Spring Road, Olney, Maryland 20832
Website: www.olneytheatre.org
This active, professional theater offers year-round programming.

POOLESVILLE PUBLIC GOLF COURSE

Address: 16601 W. Willard Road, Poolesville, Maryland 20837
Website: www.montgomerycountygolf.com
While Bernie's Club, the former Potomac Valley Lodge, is no longer open, you can stop by the golf course and play nine or eighteen holes and also see the building.

SANDY SPRING

The village of Sandy Spring is a charming area with many parks and museums. The following sites have information on how to explore the area on your own:

- Underground Railroad Experience Trail:
www.montgomeryparks.org/PPSD/Cultural_Resources_Stewardship/
heritage/urr_experience.shtm
- Sandy Spring Museum:
www.sandyspringmuseum.org
- Sandy Spring Slave Museum:
www.sandyspringslavemuseum.org

Selected Sources

Research Facilities

Chevy Chase Historical Society: Used unpublished manuscript collections, history files, and photographs. www.chevychasehistory. org

Jane C. Sween Library, Montgomery County Historical Society: Extensively used the archival, unpublished manuscripts, subject files, Montgomery Sentinel and Gazette newspapers, and photographic and map collections. www.montgomeryhistory.org

Montgomery County Historic Preservation Commission, M-NCPPC: Used subject files for historic properties. www.montgomeryparks. org/PPSD/Cultural_Resources_Stewardship

Montgomery County Public Libraries: Used the historic newspaper collections for the *Washington Star* and *Washington Post*. www. montgomerycountymd.gov/content/libraries

Sandy Spring Museum: Used subject files for properties and people from the Sandy Spring area. www.sandyspringmuseum.org

Print Sources

Atlas of Fifteen Miles Around Washington Including the County of Montgomery, Maryland. Philadelphia, Pennsylvania: G. M. Hopkins, C. E., 1879. Reprint. Rockville, Maryland: Montgomery County Historical Society, 1975.

Barrow, Healan & Kristine Stevens. *Olney: Echoes of the Past*. Reprint. Westminster, Maryland: Willow Bend Books, 2000.

Boggs, Ardith Gunderman. *Goshen, Maryland: A History & Its People*. Bowie, Maryland: Heritage Books, Inc., 1994.

Bowen, John D. *Guide to Selections from the Montgomery County Sentinel, Maryland*. Westminster, Maryland: Heritage Press (multiple volumes).

Boyd, T. H. S. *The History of Montgomery County, Maryland, From Its Earliest Settlement in 1650 to 1879*. Clarksburg, Maryland, 1879. Reprint. Baltimore, Maryland: Clearfield Company, Reprints & Remainders, 1989.

Camagna, Dorothy. *The C & O Canal, from Great National Project to National Historical Park*. Gaithersburg, Maryland: Belshore Publications, 2006.

Cavicchi, Clare Lise. *Places from the Past: The Tradition of Gardez Bien in Montgomery County, MD*. Silver Spring, Maryland: M-NCPPC, 2001.

Clark, Ella E. & Thomas F. Hahn, Editors. *Life on the Chesapeake & Ohio Canal 1859*. Shepherdstown, West Virginia: The American Canal & Transportation Center, 1975.

Cook, Richard and Deborah Lange. *Glen Echo Park: A Story of Survival*. Bethesda, Maryland: Communications Group, 2000.

Cutler, Dona and Dorothy J. Elgin. *The History of Poolesville*. Bowie, Maryland: Heritage Books, Inc., 2000.

Dwyer, Mike. *Montgomery County (Images of America Series)*. Charleston, South Carolina: Arcadia Press, 2006.

Farquhar, Roger Brooke. *Old Homes and History of Montgomery County, Maryland*. Washington, D.C.: Judd & Detweiler, 1962.

Farquhar, William Henry. *Annals of Sandy Spring or Twenty Years History in a Rural Community of Maryland*. 1884. Reprint. Cottonport, Louisiana: Polyanthus Press, 1972.

Farwell, Byron. *Ball's Bluff: A Small Battle and Its Long Shadow*. McLean, Virginia: EPM Publications, Inc., 1990.

Goetz, Walter. *Montgomery County Gold Fever*. Self-published, 1988.

Hahn, Thomas Swiftwater. *The Chesapeake and Ohio Canal Lock-Houses and Lock-Keepers*. Morgantown, West Virginia: Institute for the History of Technology and Industrial Archaeology, 1996.

Halper, Lee and Jane Freundel Levey, Eds. *Enchanted Forest Glen: The Endangered Legacy of National Park Seminary Historic District in Silver Spring, Maryland*. Silver Spring, Maryland: Save Our Seminary at Forest Glen, 1999.

Harris, Ann Paterson. *The Potomac Adventure*. Self-published, 1978.

Hiebert, Ray Eldon and Richard K. McMaster. *A Grateful Remembrance: The Story of Montgomery County, Maryland*. Rockville, Maryland: Montgomery County Government and the Montgomery County Historical Society, 1976.

High, Mike. *The C & O Canal Companion*. Baltimore, Maryland: Johns Hopkins University Press, 1997.

Holien, Kim Bernard. *Battle at Ball's Bluff*. Orange, Virginia: Moss Publications, 1985.

Hurley, William Neal. *Population Census of Montgomery County, MD*. Bowie, Maryland: Heritage Books (multiple volumes).

Ingalls, Edgar T. *The Discovery of Gold at Great Falls, Maryland, Mining and Milling*. Privately printed, 1960.

Jacobs, Charles. *Civil War Guide to Montgomery County, Maryland*. Rockville, Maryland: Montgomery County Historical Society, 1996.

Judge, Joseph. *Season of Fire: The Confederate Strike on Washington*. Berryville, Virginia: Rockbridge Publishing Company, 1994.

Lord, Walter. *The Dawn's Early Light*. New York, New York: W.W. Norton & Co., 1972.

McConihe, Margo. *History of Potomac*. Potomac, Maryland: Potomac Almanac, 1970.

McGuckian, Eileen S. *Rockville: Portrait of a City*. Franklin, Tennessee: Hillsboro Press, 2001.

Montgomery Mutual Insurance Co., unpublished archival collection, Jane C. Sween Library.

Pitch, Anthony. *"They Shot Papa Dead!" The Road to Ford's Theatre, Abraham Lincoln's Murder, and the Rage for Vengeance*. Hanover, New Hampshire: Steerforth Press, 2008.
The Burning of Washington: The British Invasion of 1814. Annapolis, Maryland: Naval Institute Press, 1998.

Rubin, Mary H. *The Chesapeake and Ohio Canal (Images of America)*. Charleston, South Carolina: Arcadia Press, 2003.

Schaffer, Rich and Ric Nelson. *Forest Glen (Images of America)*. Charleston, South Carolina: Arcadia Press, 2004.

Slave Census 1867-1868; Montgomery County, Maryland. Unpublished manuscript, MCHS-JCSL.

Smith, Margaret Bayard. *The First Forty Years of Washington Society*. London, England: T. Fisher Unwin, 1906 (Google Books).

Spears, Edward, Editor. *The Assassination of President Lincoln and the Trial of the Conspirators*. Lexington, Kentucky: The University Press of Kentucky, 2003.

Sween, Jane C. and William Offutt. *Montgomery County: Centuries of Change*. Sun Valley, California: American Historical Press, 1999.

Vlach, John Michael. *Back of the Big House: the Architecture of Plantation Slavery*. Chapel Hill, North Carolina: University of North Carolina Press, 1993.

Wahll, Andrew. *Braddock Road Chronicles 1755*. Westminster, Maryland: Heritage Books, 1999.

Walston, Mark. "A Survey of Slave Housing in Montgomery County, Maryland," *The Montgomery County Story*, Vol. 27, Number 3, Aug. 1984.

Ways, Harry C. *The Washington Aqueduct 1852-1992*. Baltimore, Maryland: US Army Corps of Engineers, Baltimore District, 1996.

Whitehorne, Joseph A. *The Battle for Baltimore 1814*. Mt. Pleasant, South Carolina: The Nautical and Aviation Publishing Co. of America, 1997.

Wolfe, George "Hooper." *I Drove Mules on the Chesapeake and Ohio Canal*. Dover, Delaware: Dover Graphic Association and Woodwend Studio of Dover, Delaware, 1969. Third printing, 1976.

Online Resources:

Battle of Ball's Bluff:
http://www.cem.va.gov/CEM/cems/nchp/ballsbluff.asp
     www.mrlincolnswhitehouse.org
     www.nvrpa.org/parks/ballsbluff
     www.nps.gov/prsf/

Goshen Mennonite Church: www.goshenmennonite.org/history.html

Little Bennett Regional Park:
http://www.littlebennettcampground.com
     www.montgomerytrails.org
     www.parkhistoricsites.org

Library of Congress, Historic American Buildings Survey/Historic American Engineering Record/Historic American Landscapes Survey: www.loc.gov/pictures/collection/hh

Maryland Inventory of Historic Properties: http://www.mdihp.net/.

Montgomery County Historic Preservation Commission:
www.montgomeryplanning.org/historic

Index